What a splendid book! I praise God for this great resource. This book provides useful tools for people reading Mark's Gospel and so also the other Gospels. If people are going to read the Bible, they need to be trained to understand it deeply. This book will also be a great resource for Bible study leaders and preachers. I am only sorry that I had not read this book before preaching a recent series on Mark!
Peter Adam, Vicar Emeritus of St Jude's Carlton, Melbourne, Australia

This book is a gold mine, not just because of the many rich ideas it contains, but especially because it enables us to discover the treasures of the Gospels. It is a fantastic addition to the *Dig Deeper* series, and is hugely valuable as a model of how to study a Bible book so as to embrace its message and be transformed by its power. The Toolkit is brilliant, the writing is clear and accessible, the interactive questions are penetrating, and the resulting engagement with the Gospel – with Jesus himself – is compelling and life-changing. Whether for personal use, home groups or preparing to preach, I urgently encourage you to dig into this wonderful guide to Mark's Gospel.
Jonathan Lamb, CEO and minister-at-large for Keswick Ministries, formerly Director of Langham Preaching

Commenting on the sister volume *Dig Even Deeper*:
Dig Even Deeper is gold! It's a resource that will introduce even the newest Bible reader to thinking deeply about the message of the Bible . . . I'm looking forward to introducing it to all our Bible study programmes.
Nick Drake, Pastor, Campus Church, University of Canterbury, New Zealand

DIG
DEEPER
into the
GOSPELS

Andrew Sach & Tim Hiorns

DIG
DEEPER
into the
GOSPELS

Coming face to face with Jesus in Mark

ivp

INTER-VARSITY PRESS
Norton Street, Nottingham NG7 3HR, England
Email: ivp@ivpbooks.com
Website: www.ivpbooks.com

British Library Cataloguing in Publication Data
A catalogue record for this book is available from the British Library.

ISBN: 978-1-78359-199-2

Set in Dante 12/15pt
Typeset in Great Britain by CRB Associates, Potterhanworth, Lincolnshire
Printed in Great Britain by Ashford Colour Press Ltd, Gosport, Hampshire

Inter-Varsity Press publishes Christian books that are true to the Bible and that communicate the gospel, develop discipleship and strengthen the church for its mission in the world.

Inter-Varsity Press is closely linked with the Universities and Colleges Christian Fellowship, a student movement connecting Christian Unions in universities and colleges throughout Great Britain, and a member movement of the International Fellowship of Evangelical Students. Website: www.uccf.org.uk

Dedication

To Tim's wife, Lucy, and
to Andrew's goddaughter, Imogen,
who have denied themselves,
taken up their crosses and
followed Jesus (Mark 8:34).

'BLESSED Lord, who hast caused all holy Scriptures
to be written for our learning: Grant that we may
in such wise hear them, read, mark, learn, and
inwardly digest them, that by patience and comfort
of thy holy Word, we may embrace and ever hold fast
the blessed hope of everlasting life, which thou hast
given us in our Saviour Jesus Christ. Amen.'
(Book of Common Prayer, 1662)

Contents

Acknowledgments

As we've dug deeper into Mark's Gospel, we've been very aware that we weren't the only ones holding spades. Thanks to all those who've partnered in the 'Read Mark Learn' studies at St Helen's, Bishopsgate, especially Amy Wicks, Aneirin Glyn, Charlie Skrine and Jamie Child. Thanks to Matthew Sleeman at Oak Hill for pointing us to some more scholarly material, for example, Rikki Watts on Mark's use of Isaiah's use of Exodus. Thanks to those who wrote the commentaries we regularly consulted (although we didn't always agree with you): Bolt, Calvin, Edwards, France, Hooker, Horne, Lane, van Iersel, Witherington III. And to Chris Thomson and Thomas Renz for offering scholarly advice on Old Testament questions.

Thanks to all of our friends who mocked us with suggested titles, following on from *Dig Deeper* and *Dig Even Deeper*. Sorry that *Rock Bottom* didn't make the cut this time round!

Thanks to those who took part in the spoof Mark 13 sketch, and Philip Brentford who was had; Dave Bignell for his inflatable ears; James Brabner and Stefan Davies for help foraging in Croatia; Caroline Newton for her Dulux tester pot analogy; Mike Ovey for the image of 'unscrewing tiny light bulbs'; Anna Watkin for telling us about bowls of water on Chinese buses; Flic Carswell for brushing up her Shakespeare;

Ali Elmore for providing regular encouragement of an edible kind.

Thanks to Nigel Beynon and Rich Alldritt who helped develop the Dig Deeper concept. To Claire 'spot-a-split-infinitive-at-100-paces' Tunks, Andrew Grey and Andy Carruthers for reading the manuscript. To William Taylor for his teaching and example that always underlines the power and sufficiency of the Word of God.

Thanks to the wonderful Eleanor Trotter, editor at IVP, who responded with such good humour to our graph of 'current word count vs. editor's dream word count'. (The book was in danger of being *much* longer.)

Thanks (from Tim in particular!) to Lucy, for being such a loving, supportive and funny wife. Your constant desire for us to root our lives in God's Word is such a blessing.

Thanks to Square Mile Roasters. Nude Espresso. Has Bean Coffee. The Monmouth Coffee Company. The Wren Café.

Thanks to God the Father. You know we've often asked for your help in the writing of this book, and we're so grateful for the grace you've given us to complete it. Thanks to God the Son. You gave your life to pay our ransom. We ask that this book would lead to the honour of your name in the lives of all who read it. Thanks to God the Holy Spirit. You breathed out the life-changing words of Mark's Gospel, and opened our eyes to see Jesus.

Getting started

Making a cup of coffee – how hard can it be? Any child old enough to be trusted with a kettle can manage it. Boil water. Add Nescafé. Serve.

This was my (Tim's) attitude until I arrived at Andrew's house for our first session working on this book. It takes him at least fifteen minutes to grind the beans, froth the milk, extract the espresso and try to pour a Rosetta (he even has an app on his iPhone complete with tutorial videos). I do question whether it's necessary to hit a brew temperature of exactly 94.5°, or whether the taste would be altered that much if the extraction time dipped below the recommended twenty-five seconds, but what do I know? Andrew assures me that there is much more to coffee than I think.

The same is true of Mark's Gospel.

When it comes to the Gospels, many of us have a boil-water-add-Nescafé-serve mentality. Any child who's been through Sunday school can tell you that Jesus walked on water, fed the 5,000 and told a parable about a sower. And so we tend to think of the Gospels as the 'easy' bits of the Bible, in contrast to something like Romans or Isaiah, and seldom give them the time or serious thought that they deserve. That's a real shame.

The fact is, Mark's sixteen brief chapters narrate the most important things that have ever happened in the history of the world. And being a theologian as well as a historian, Mark tells us what those events mean. We shall discover a diagnosis of the human condition more perceptive than those offered by any modern physician, politician, philosopher or psychiatrist. We shall read of a solution that touches, in the same moment, both the horror of hell and the glory of heaven. We shall come face to face with the most powerful, compassionate, frightening, courageous, loving human being ever to have lived. We shall be taught how to follow him in a way that will utterly transform our lives.

The conviction behind the *Dig Deeper* books is that there is more to discover in God's Word if we are prepared to put some effort in, like the 'unashamed workman' of 2 Timothy 2:15. The rewards are incredible. We've now studied Mark for a total of eleven years between us (we work through it every year with newcomers at our church), and we keep learning new things, getting clearer, refining our understanding. It's been one of the greatest blessings of our Christian lives to see Jesus in the Gospels *as he actually is*.

How do we go about reading the Gospels rightly? First, we need to acknowledge our dependence on the Holy Spirit. He is the one who 'breathed out' the Scriptures in the first place (2 Timothy 3:16; 2 Peter 1:21), and he brings them to bear on our lives with power today (Ephesians 6:17; 1 Thessalonians 1:5). Studying the Bible is a profoundly spiritual experience. Those who realize this will be often on their knees in prayer.

Secondly, we need to be willing to make the lifestyle changes that Jesus asks of us. Obedience leads to clarity, whereas hard-heartedness leads to confusion (as Mark himself will show us). The theology professor who loves money and sleeps with her boyfriend will understand the Bible half as well as the illiterate who takes Jesus' words to heart and does them.

Thirdly, we can benefit from knowing (and becoming skilled in the use of) various Bible-handling 'tools'. The Bible Toolkit was first introduced in the original *Dig Deeper* (2005), where we devoted one chapter to each of sixteen principles that can be used with any Bible passage – you'll find a summary at the end of this book. As we work through Mark's Gospel, we shall find the tools invaluable in discovering truths we might otherwise miss. The **Structure tool** will help us understand why Jesus got angry with a fig tree (11:12–14); the **Context tool** will explain why a request for an exorcism turned into a conversation about bread (7:24–29); the **Quotation/Allusion tool** will show us what walking on water and feeding 5,000 have in common. And so on.

In *Dig Even Deeper* (2010), the toolkit went 'live' on the book of Exodus, and now we're tackling Mark. Why all these sequels? Simply because it's one thing to know that a saw cuts wood, and quite another to be able to make a kitchen cabinet. Or a violin. You don't need every tool for every job, and knowing which tool to use when is often a matter of judgment. This can only come with practice. Also, just as violin-making might require a slightly different use of the saw from cabinet-making, so we shall need to approach Mark's Gospel a bit differently from how we handled Exodus. If the series continues, we hope to explore even more types of Bible literature – for example, an Old Testament prophet or a New Testament letter.

As you read this book, we hope first and foremost that you will grow to know Jesus better. That you will understand the implications of his glorious death and resurrection. That you will be motivated and equipped to follow him more closely. But we also pray that you'll become a more able and confident

Bible student. That, having looked over our shoulder and watched us work away at Mark, you'll be able to take these same tools elsewhere and mine for yourself the treasures of the Gospel of Matthew or Luke or John (or even Malachi or Leviticus or Jeremiah!).

Getting the most out of this book

Dig Deeper into the Gospels is designed to be an interactive experience, and to that end we've included exercises in most chapters, so that you can practise using the tools for yourself.

Your first assignment is this: close *Dig Deeper into the Gospels*, written on an Apple Mac by a couple of blokes in East London, and pick up the Gospel of Mark, written under the inspiration of the Holy Spirit of God. It should be obvious which is the more important. Read it from cover to cover. Even better, read it from cover to cover twice. Or read it once for yourself, and then listen to one of those audio Bibles available on the internet. (You might need to shop around if you can't handle cringey background music and over-ambitious attempts to render sound effects.) Don't worry about understanding all the details at this stage; the aim is simply to increase your familiarity with the text and to help you start to notice some of the big repeated ideas. When it comes to serious Bible study, there is no substitute for reading and rereading, and rereading again.

Read Mark now before turning over. We should warn you that there will be a little test over the page!

Welcome back. Feeling more familiar with Mark's Gospel? As a bit of fun, we set our Bible study leaders at St Helen's a test at the beginning of the year. We thought you might enjoy it too, so here it is.

1. Who calls Jesus the 'Christ' or the 'Son of God'? (There is more than one correct answer.)
2. Complete the verse: 'If anyone would come after me, let him deny himself . . .'
3. The number twelve crops up a few times in Mark. But what different things are there twelve of?
4. Which of the following is not found in Mark's Gospel?
   a) 'But now let the one who has a moneybag take it, and likewise a knapsack.'
   b) 'Truly I say to you, whoever gives you a cup of water to drink because you belong to Christ will by no means lose his reward.'
   c) He could do no mighty work there, except that he laid his hands on a few sick people and healed them.
5. List all the animals mentioned in Mark's Gospel (more than you think!)

You'll find the answers at the back of this book.

The overall shape of Mark's Gospel

Before we dive into Mark chapter 1, it's helpful to have the overall shape of the Gospel clear in our minds. Cue the **Structure tool**.

The moment when Peter confesses, 'You are the Christ' (8:29) is an obvious turning point. It's taken eight chapters of teaching about Jesus' identity for the penny to drop, but finally Peter gets it. Immediately after this, Jesus begins to emphasize a new theme: 'the Son of Man must suffer many things . . .' (8:31), and the countdown begins to his death and resurrection. Seeing Peter's confession as a kind of hinge, people have often divided the Gospel into two halves:

- Chapters 1 – 8: Who is Jesus?
- Chapters 9 – 16: Why did Jesus come?

This is helpful as long as we don't push it too far. There are references to why Jesus came also in the *first* half of the Gospel (e.g. 2:17), and the question of his identity continues to rumble on in the second half (e.g. 12:35–37; 14:61–63). Nonetheless, Peter's confession deserves a place in our overall structure.

But we can't really talk about *Peter's* confession without also talking about the *centurion's* confession: 'Truly this man was the Son of God!' (15:39). Significantly, these are the two moments in the Gospel that Mark has chosen to flag up in his opening sentence (1:1, which we like to call *Mark's* confession):

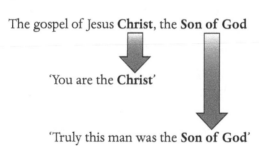

The gospel of Jesus **Christ**, the **Son of God**

'You are the **Christ**'

'Truly this man was the **Son of God**'

Clustered around these three confessions are various other unique details that confirm that Mark wants us to link them together. For example, the first and third confessions are marked by things being 'torn' by God (the heavens in 1:10; the temple curtain in 15:38), by references to people 'ministering' to Jesus (angels in 1:13; women in 15:41), and by people 'crying' out (a prophetic voice in 1:3; Jesus in 15:34). The first and second confessions are connected by almost identical proclamations from heaven ('You are my beloved Son' in 1:11; 'This is my beloved Son' in 9:7). The second and third confessions are connected by white clothing (the glorified Jesus in 9:3; a messenger from the glorified Jesus in 16:5).

Please don't worry if you wouldn't have spotted all of these things yourself. We didn't either! We just thought it was worth giving you a glimpse early on of just how sophisticated a writer Mark can be. He could have said that the heavens were 'opened', but he chooses to say 'torn open' for a reason. It makes a difference to how you read something, knowing that the author has carefully chosen every *word*.

To summarize where we've got to, Mark has structured his whole Gospel around the titles: 'Christ' and 'Son of God'. Establishing Jesus' identity is central to his purpose.

But we're not finished with the **Structure tool** yet. Bible authors will often mark out a section by topping and tailing it with two similar incidents, like a pair of bookends. We wondered whether this was what Mark was doing with the two stories of blind men receiving sight in 8:22–26 and 10:46–52. Of course, we can't give bookend status to every pair of incidents that happen to share a few similarities. John's camel-hair fashion statement (1:6) and Jesus' camel-through-the-eye-of-a-needle image (10:25) are not meant to be linked. When we spot potential bookends, we need to look at the material in between and see whether it makes sense for it to be a section. The between-camels verses don't. The between-blind-men verses do.

Between the blind-men bookends, Jesus' teaching has a particular focus. Three times he predicts that 'the Son of Man' will be killed and after three days rise again (Mark 8:31; 9:31; 10:32–34). Each time this is followed by instructions on discipleship, as Jesus explains what it means to deny ourselves, take up our own cross and follow him. We might call this the 'cross-shaped life' section.

There is also a hint that Mark intends to distinguish the sections geographically. Before the first blind man, most of the action takes place in Galilee in the north. After the second blind man, we enter Jerusalem in the south. In between, Mark tells us five times that they are 'on the way' (8:27; 9:33, 34; 10:32, 52).[1] It's a clever phrase, because it combines an emphasis on Jesus' destiny (he's on his way to his death) with a challenge to discipleship (will you follow him on the way?).

There is one final observation to make before we draw everything together, and it involves the **Genre tool**. For most of the Gospel, it is the narrator's voice that we are listening to, with occasional speech bubbles from others. But chapter 4 is (almost) one big speech bubble. And so is chapter 13. Why has Mark chosen to give us two full-length sermons from Jesus at exactly these places in the story? That is something we'll need to keep in mind.

If ever there was a need to draw a giant diagram, this is it.

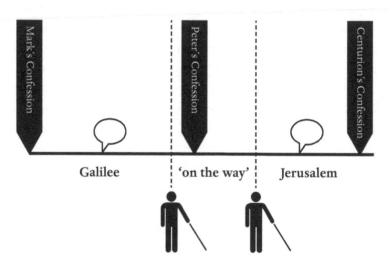

The *Columbo* moment (1:1–15)

Because we're working quite closely with the Bible text, you'll want to have a Bible open. Now is a good time to reread 1:1–15.

Jesus is God's King

Remember the American television show, *Columbo*? It was daytime TV in the 1980s, and I (Andrew) always looked forward to it on sick days. Tim has never seen it because he's too young, and wouldn't have been allowed to anyway, because doctors' kids can't miss school for anything less than heart surgery.

Columbo was a classic detective show with a difference. Usually, the identity of the murderer is not revealed until the climax of the story, but in *Columbo* we find out 'whodunit' in the first five minutes. The enjoyment (or frustration) of the rest of the episode comes from watching our hero figure it out.

Similarly, in his Gospel, Mark tells us the punchline up front: 'the gospel of Jesus Christ, the Son of God' (1:1). And then, in true *Columbo* style, we spend the rest of the Gospel waiting for Jesus' followers to discover the truth.

But what exactly is Mark's opening sentence telling us about Jesus? People might think of 'Christ' as Jesus' surname, as if Mr and Mrs Christ had a son, but the **Vocabulary tool** tells us (e.g. by looking up 'Christ' in a dictionary) that Christ is the Greek translation of the Hebrew word *Messiah*, meaning God's anointed King. Similarly, 'Son of God' is one of the ways that the Old Testament spoke of the King who was to come:

> I will establish the throne of his kingdom for ever. I will be to him a father, and he shall be to me a son.
> (2 Samuel 7:13-14)

> I have set my King
>   on Zion, my holy hill . . .
> 'You are my Son;
>   today I have begotten you.'
> (Psalm 2:6-7)

So, by using both titles, 'Christ' and 'Son of God' together, Mark has really told us the same thing twice. We could paraphrase: 'the beginning of the gospel of Jesus the King, the King'.

Lots of different things happen in the first few paragraphs following this introduction. We're told about a man called John and his odd dietary habits; there's a baptism; Jesus hangs out with a strange crowd in the wilderness; good news is preached in Galilee. But the **Structure tool** helps us to see that it all belongs together, and makes a single point. How? As we shall find him doing again and again, Mark encloses the mini-section in a pair of bookends that match each other. Verse 1 spoke of the gospel about a King. Verses 14-15 announce the gospel about a kingdom. Somehow the whole opening section is intended to convince us of the good news that the King(dom) has arrived.

To begin with, Mark takes us to the Old Testament to remind us that the King would not turn up unannounced: first there would come a 'messenger' or 'voice' to prepare the way. It's a bit like when a celebrity comes to town. Before you see the limousine with blacked-out windows, you get (if the celebrity is important enough) a police outrider going on ahead, stopping the traffic. It would be strange for the front page of the tabloids to carry a photo of the outrider; he's hardly the star of the show. But in this case, Mark spends five verses telling us about him. His logic seems to be this: 'If I can convince them that John the Baptist is the outrider mentioned by Isaiah, then I'll get their hearts beating faster as they realize who is expected next on the scene.'

If we read Mark's description of John in isolation, we are at a loss to make sense of the details. But when we use the **Context tool**, we find that almost every feature of vv. 4–8 corresponds to something in the prophecy of vv. 2–3:

Prophecy (vv. 2–3)	How Mark convinces us that John is the perfect fit (vv. 4–8)
The forerunner is described as a 'messenger' or 'voice' – his role is to speak.	Mark goes out of his way to describe John's ministry not simply as 'baptizing', but also '*proclaiming* a baptism'.
The forerunner can be found 'in the wilderness'.	John's ministry took place 'in the wilderness'.
The forerunner is there to '[p]repare the way' for someone.	John is pointing to the one who comes 'after me'.
?	'John was clothed with camel's hair and wore a leather belt around his waist.'

The bottom row of the table is the trickiest, but that's just because we know the Bible less well than *Superman* films. Let us explain . . . if you saw someone with underpants on the outside of his trousers and a big red-and-yellow 'S' on his front, you'd have no difficulty figuring out who he was dressed as. Similarly, the camel's-hair tunic and leather belt ensemble would have been instantly recognizable by a first-century Jew who knew their Old Testament. Time for you to do some work for yourself, with the help of the **Quotation/Allusion tool.**

DIG DEEPER: **Quotation/Allusion tool**

The first half of Mark's quote comes from Malachi 3:1, which is part of a longer prophecy about the coming of the Lord and the messenger who precedes him. Look up Malachi 4:5 to find out the name of this messenger.

Look up 2 Kings 1:7–8 to find out what the guy with this name was famous for wearing. Bingo!

In all of these different ways, then, Mark is showing us that John the Baptist fits the profile of Malachi's 'messenger' or Isaiah's 'voice'. According to v. 5, 'all the country of Judea and all Jerusalem were going out to him', and the popularity of his ministry is noted by the first-century Jewish historian Josephus (*Antiquities* 18.5.2). But John the Baptist doesn't want the limelight for himself. He is only the outrider. In starkly self-effacing terms, he insists that he is not worthy to untie Jesus' shoelaces (v. 7). He protests that his ministry is, in comparison with the powerful reality of Jesus' Holy Spirit baptism, nothing more than making people wet (v. 8). In every way he points away from himself to the one who is to come after him.

Jesus is God's King. The voice in the wilderness proclaims it.

Next, Mark takes us to the baptism of Jesus. Two details of the account underline Jesus' identity. The first is the 'Spirit descending on him like a dove' (v. 10). Two verses earlier (**Context tool**), John had told us that the coming one would baptize with the Holy Spirit, and the visible descent of the Spirit on Jesus unmistakably identifies him: he receives the Spirit that he might baptize others in the Spirit.

The second detail is the message that God the Father shouts from heaven: 'You are my beloved Son; with you I am well pleased' (v. 11). We've already mentioned that 'Son of God' is a kingly title, but here we have it from the lips of the Creator himself. It's not often that God makes an announcement over the heavenly tannoy. This is another way of telling us that the arrival of Jesus is a really, really big deal.

Jesus is God's King. The voice from heaven shouts it.

Next, the Spirit thrusts Jesus into the wilderness where he is with the wild animals (vv. 12–13). But it's not a typical David Attenborough BBC wildlife scene, because alongside the lions and rock badgers, we find Satan tempting Jesus, and angels serving him. Jesus' arrival is accompanied by spiritual activity of most unusual intensity.

Jesus is God's King. The spiritual powers recognize it.

Finally, Jesus arrives in Galilee to begin his public ministry. It would be rather arrogant to turn up at a social gathering and announce, as you walk through the door, 'The party can get started now!' But that is exactly what Jesus does. 'The kingdom of God is at hand,' he says (v. 15). 'I'm here.'

Jesus is God's King. His own preaching emphasizes it.

Jesus has come to save

If we were digging deep enough for, say, a one-storey extension, we would stop there. But let's keep on and see if we can go further with v. 13. In our reading of what other people have said about Mark's Gospel, we came across a number of interpretations of the phrase: 'he was with the wild animals':

1. The 'Jesus-knows-what-you're-going-through' theory. The Roman historian, Tacitus, records that Christians persecuted by Nero in the 60s AD were 'covered with the hides of wild beasts and torn to pieces by dogs' (*Annals* 15.44). By mentioning that Jesus also faced the threat of wild animals, Mark is telling his early readers that Jesus can identify with them in their suffering.
2. The 'Jesus-is-greater-than-Nebuchadnezzar' theory. The suggestion is that Jesus' experience parallels the fate of the Babylonian king described in Daniel 4:28–37, who spends time in the wilderness with wild animals, wet with dew (just as Jesus would have been wet following his baptism).[1]

The fatal flaw in these interpretations is that *Mark himself suggests neither of them*. In other words, they fall foul of the **Author's Purpose tool**, the most important tool of them all.

If we are using the **Author's Purpose tool** correctly, we are not at liberty to draw our own biblical or theological connections from ideas that Mark mentions: 'Here is a mention of wild animals, and so that could mean . . .', and off we go into Daniel or Tacitus or wherever. Instead, we should look for the connections that Mark explicitly draws. One of our friends explains this using the analogy of a game of dot-to-dot. See below two attempts by kids at our church. The child on the left makes use of some of the dots, but connects them in her own delightfully imaginative way. The child on the right, by following the numbers, gets the author's intended connection between the dots. The pictures that emerge are quite different.

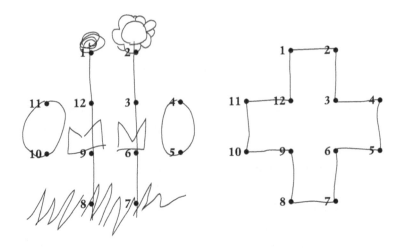

What then, if any, are Mark's own clues about how to interpret Jesus' forty-day safari in the wilderness? We've noticed already that the angels in attendance point to his kingly majesty. But is there more that can be said?

As always, we need to look closely at the text, and when we do so, we find that it reads rather strangely: 'The Spirit immediately drove him out into the wilderness. And he was in the wilderness . . .' (vv. 12–13). Why say it twice? You would never say, 'I went to Bristol. And I was in Bristol.' It seems that the location is especially important to Mark, and the **Context tool** shows us why. For it was 'in the wilderness' that Isaiah had said a voice would cry out (v. 3), and 'in the wilderness' that John appeared baptizing (v. 4). By reusing that phrase, Mark is showing us that it is Isaiah and John (not Nero or Nebuchadnezzar) who will help us join the dots correctly.

Isaiah was writing just before the Israelites went into exile in Babylon because of their sin. Against a backdrop of doom and judgment, his 'voice crying in the wilderness' announces rescue and forgiveness.

John's ministry in the wilderness was all about forgiveness too. He preached 'a baptism of repentance for the forgiveness of sins' (v. 4), and as people were baptized, they were 'confessing their sins' (v. 5). But washing with water couldn't wash the heart; only the baptism of the Holy Spirit could achieve that.

And so Jesus is driven into the wilderness. Having done the work using the **Context tool**, the significance of this desert location is abundantly clear: Jesus has come to do the thing that Isaiah prophesied and John's baptism symbolized. He has come to bring forgiveness.[2]

It's nice that once you lock on to the author's purpose, even the little details start to slot into place. As we were reading through the 'salvation in the wilderness' section of Isaiah, we found that it centres on a servant whom God delights in and puts his Spirit upon (42:1) – we couldn't help thinking of the dove and the heavenly commendation at Jesus' baptism. Then we found that God promised to pour out his Spirit on his people – we couldn't help thinking of John's promise that Jesus would baptize with the Spirit. We *even* found wild animals honouring God (43:20)! As for the forty days, if the wilderness in Isaiah was symbolically the place that sin takes you to, and from which you need deliverance, then the most obvious parallel is the forty years of wandering in the desert earlier in Israel's history (see Numbers 14:34).

Jesus has come to save.

The *Columbo* experience

We've come a long way in our understanding of Mark 1:1–15. But how should it affect us today? How ought we to respond? In one sense, we have not understood any part of the Bible until we can answer that question.

Fortunately, Jesus tells us exactly what response is required (v. 15). Direct imperatives can be a real help when we're using the **'So What?' tool**.[3] If you're not a grammar boffin, and you don't know an imperative from an indicative, think back to your driving theory test. You'll remember that in the Highway Code, information signs are often rectangular: 'The next Motorway Services has a KFC', while warning signs come in red triangles: 'Road narrows on both sides', and signs giving orders come in a blue or red circle: 'Keep left' or 'No entry'. The imperatives are the circle ones. They are the places where we are told exactly what to do and not do. And here is one such case: 'repent and believe in the gospel.'

To return to our *Columbo* analogy, we now know whodunit. And we know what he dun! And we know what we need to do! But we're only five minutes in, and we have the whole of the show to look forward to. Mark is going to take the best part of sixteen chapters to help us get our heads around it, understand it deeply, have it more profoundly grip and move us. What kind of 'King' is Jesus anyway? What will his kingdom be like? How will he save people? Do they really need saving? What does it mean to repent? How radical does that need to be? Is it worth it?

Why not spend some time in prayer before you turn the page?

Heavenly Father, thank you that Jesus is your King, whom you promised hundreds of years beforehand through the prophet Isaiah, and prepared for through your servant John the Baptist. Thank you for that day in history when you tore open the heavens to shout down how delighted you were with him. Thank you that he came on a mission to save us from the wilderness where our sin had taken us. Help us to turn to him in repentance, and to trust him. We pray that your Holy Spirit who inspired Mark to write this Gospel will be at work powerfully in us as we read the chapters ahead. In Jesus' name. Amen.

The kingdom colours (1:16 – 2:17)

Hands up anyone who has ever bought something online that didn't quite match up to expectations. Andrew thinks painfully of the 'ultrasonic glasses cleaner' that turned out to be a bowl of water that rattled. Or the 'ultra-bright reflective material' for safer cycling that was considerably less reflective than a sheet of A4 paper. Or the . . . (many other possible stories that will have to be left for another time). Tim, on the other hand, is a less gullible consumer. Rather than relying exclusively on the manufacturers' descriptions, he likes to check the feedback that other buyers have given.

When it comes to the kingdom of God, there are plenty of amazing descriptions 'in the catalogue', as it were. Isaiah describes it as a great banquet at which God will 'swallow up death forever; and . . . wipe away tears from all faces' (Isaiah 25:6–8), or as a time when:

> . . . the eyes of the blind shall be opened,
>   and the ears of the deaf unstopped;
> then shall the lame man leap like a deer,
>   and the tongue of the mute sing for joy.
> (Isaiah 35:5–6)

But what if it doesn't match up to expectations? Of course, Isaiah is more trustworthy than an internet salesman. He is God's prophet, and so we have every reason to take him at his word. But our faith is weak, and his promise of a perfect kingdom can seem remote and intangible. If only we had some 'user feedback'. If only we could read eyewitness testimonies of those who had actually experienced these things first-hand. And . . . we can. That is exactly what we have in Mark 1:16 – 2:17! (Remember, we're expecting you to have a Bible open and to read the relevant verses before you read what we have to say.)

The **Structure tool** is usually the best place to start. We've spoken already about Mark's use of bookends to define a section, and we've found some here. Double bookends in fact!

> BOOKEND A: Jesus passes beside the sea. He sees Simon and Andrew, James and John, busy at work. He calls them, and they follow (1:16–20).
> BOOKEND B: Jesus is teaching in a synagogue in Capernaum. An exorcism is seen as proof of the authority of his words (1:21–28).
> C: Stuff in between (1:29–45).
> BOOKEND B: Jesus is teaching in a house in Capernaum. A healing is seen as proof of the authority of his words (2:1–12).
> BOOKEND A: Jesus again passes beside the sea. He sees Levi, busy at work. Jesus calls him, and he follows (2:13–14).

A friend of ours was concerned that such an intricate structure might discourage you, in an 'I-would-never-have-got-that-for-myself' kind of way. But we want to reply, 'Don't be so sure.' You probably wouldn't spot it on first reading. But on a third or fourth reading, you might well begin to notice 'authority' (1:22) and 'authority' (2:10), both in Capernaum. And you start to wonder, 'Are these bookends perhaps?' And then you find 'Follow me' (1:17) and 'Follow me' (2:14), both at the seaside, and before long you've got the whole ABCBA structure mapped out. The whole point of the *Dig Deeper* books is that there is more to find in the Bible if you . . . dig deeper!

But what's the cash value in noticing a pretty ABCBA pattern? Does it help us to know God better? Actually yes, because understanding the structure is often key to understanding the author's purpose, and the author's purpose is the Holy Spirit's purpose, and the Holy Spirit wants to transform us into God's image! By bracketing everything between two demonstrations of Jesus' authority (the 'B' bookends), Mark highlights authority as a key idea. By enclosing this in a further set of bookends (the 'A' ones) in which people leave everything to follow Jesus, Mark points us to the appropriate response to this authority.

God's kingdom and evil

Let's dive in at 1:21 (we'll leave the first 'A' bookend until a bit later). Jesus is teaching in the synagogue one Sabbath when he is interrupted by a shriek from a demon-possessed man (v. 23). This sounds fantastical to some modern readers, who accuse Mark of naively misdiagnosing schizophrenia. But it is they who are naive about spiritual realities. We live in a time and a culture where much of Satan's work is behind the scenes, but when God's King walked the earth, the forces of evil broke their cover and came out to meet him. Evil is very real. But Jesus defeats it very easily – it takes him all of seven words (v. 25).

In v. 27, the people's response isn't quite as we might expect (and it's always worth pausing to look again whenever the text surprises us). Instead of 'What is this? A powerful exorcism!', the people's amazement centres instead on the authority of Jesus' *words*:

> . . . they questioned among themselves, saying, 'What is this? A new teaching with authority! He commands even the unclean spirits, and they obey him.'

It seems that the driving out of the demon is not a separate thing from the preaching that it interrupted in vv. 21–22, but an outworking of it. This makes even more sense if we use the **Context tool** to remind ourselves of the content of Jesus' message: 'The time is fulfilled, and the kingdom of God is at hand' (1:15). As Jesus announces the arrival of his kingdom, the exorcism becomes a visual demonstration of what that kingdom is like.

In God's kingdom there is no place for evil.

God's kingdom and sickness

Then Jesus starts healing people. It begins with Simon's mother-in-law in bed with a fever. By evening 'the whole city was gathered together at the door. And [Jesus] healed many who were sick with various diseases' (1:33–34).

Just imagine what that would look like today. If, instead of Capernaum, it were Cambridge. Ambulances begin to ferry patients from Addenbrooke's Hospital to the house where Jesus is staying. Entering the house is a queue of people with all sorts of debilitating conditions; leaving the house is a joyful procession of healthy people. The young footballer with the compound fracture, now bounding along the street; the grandmother with dementia recognizing her son for the first time in months; the parents of the child with leukaemia, weeping tears of relief at their daughter's restored health. The traffic on the M11, safe to say, would be a nightmare. Within hours, every flight into Stansted would be fully booked. It wouldn't matter how many channels you had on your digibox; they would all be showing the same news.

Why, then, just as Jesus' healing ministry is flourishing, does he sneak off early in the morning and announce his intention to move on to other towns to preach there (v. 38)? One interpretation drives a wedge between healing and preaching, so that we might paraphrase, 'I came to preach *and not to heal.*' But the problem is that Jesus doesn't actually say that. What's more, he goes on healing people on a massive scale (see e.g. 3:7–12 and 6:53–56). All Jesus says explicitly in v. 38 is that he wants the message of the kingdom to spread beyond Capernaum.

Rather than divorcing preaching and healing, it makes better sense to see them as connected. As it turns out, our earlier work on the structure helps here. In the first 'B' bookend, the exorcism was seen as evidence for the 'authority' of Jesus' words. In the second 'B' bookend, a healing performs exactly the same function, as the **Linking Words tool** makes clear. The reason why Jesus cures a man of his paralysis is 'that you may know that the Son of Man has authority on earth to forgive sins' (2:10). The miraculous healing authenticates the preached Word.

This raises a difficult issue, however. Why aren't Christians today emptying the hospitals in Cambridge, in Jesus' name? Or why, for that matter, do Christians still die of cancer? Are we to conclude that they are not members of the kingdom of God, or that they lack enough faith to claim the healing that Jesus offers them? Of course not. While the Bible teaches elsewhere that God can and does heal today (e.g. 1 Corinthians 12:9; James 5:14–16), nowhere does it teach us to expect hospital-emptying miracles on the scale of what happened in

Capernaum. Those belonged uniquely to the time in history when God's King walked the earth and gave us a brief glimpse of what his kingdom will be like.

One of our friends gives the analogy of decorating your house. Suppose you get a bit bored with the 1970s flowery wallpaper, and consider painting over the whole thing in Dulux 'Dusted Fondant' (yes, that really is one of their colours!). Wisely, you first buy a 'tester pot'. The idea is that you paint a small area to get a feel for what it will look like, before slapping it on wall-to-wall. What happened in Capernaum in the first century was like a tester-pot preview of the kingdom colours. No sickness, no suffering, no tears. Meanwhile, the rest of the world is still decked in the horrid flowery wallpaper: lies, lusts, leukaemia. By looking at Capernaum, through the testimony of the eyewitnesses, we get a feel for what it will be like on the day that Jesus returns, when we shall experience the kingdom 'wall-to-wall'.

In God's kingdom there is no place for sickness.

God's kingdom and sin

Next, Mark tells us in some detail about the healing of a man with leprosy. Why do we need to know about this particular miracle when we've already seen a whole town being healed? Time for you guys to do some work.

DIG DEEPER: **Quotation/Allusion tool**

Jesus' instruction to 'offer for your cleansing what Moses commanded' (1:44) is referring back to instructions given in Leviticus 14, part of the Old Testament Law.

Read Leviticus 14:1–32.

- What clues can you find that a healing from leprosy involves something more than the merely physical?
- What is significant about the name of the sacrifice(s) involving the lamb(s)?
- How are the priests' actions described in vv. 18–20 (three times) and vv. 29–31 (twice)?

What does Jesus' willingness to heal a leper teach us about his kingdom?

Let's use the **Vocabulary tool** to consider the unusual language used in Jesus' conversation with the leper. Rather than asking to be made 'well', the leper asks to be made 'clean'. The best way to understand the author's choice of a particular word is to look at how he uses that word elsewhere, and in the immediate context, Mark has spoken of an 'unclean' spirit (1:23), meaning an evil spirit or demon. The language of clean and unclean, then, is about more than physical disease. It's about contamination with sin and evil. When Jesus cleanses a leper, he is pointing to his ability and willingness to bring atonement as well as healing, forgiveness as well as cure. (Hopefully you discovered something similar in the Dig Deeper exercise, by another route.)

We know that we're on track with the author's purpose, because this connection between physical and spiritual illness comes twice more. It explains Jesus' startling response to the paralytic – 'Son, your sins are forgiven' (2:5) – when presumably his friends have gone to the trouble of digging a hole in the roof with something else in mind. You can imagine Peter whispering in Jesus' ear, 'Master, I know it's been a long day and you must be tired, but I think this one is here about his legs.' Later, of course, Jesus does heal the man of his paralysis, as a testimony for the Pharisees. But first, he deals with the underlying problem of the man's sin.

The connection between healing and forgiveness is also made at Levi's dinner party, when Jesus uses the language of medicine to explain his ministry among the spiritually ill:

> Those who are well have no need of a physician, but those who are sick. I came not to call the righteous, but sinners.
>
> (2:17)

We need to take care here. Jesus is not saying that a disabled person equals an especially sinful person. *Sometimes* in the Bible, an individual's sickness or suffering is a consequence of that same individual's sin (e.g. Numbers 12:9–10; 2 Chronicles 26:16–21; 1 Corinthians 11:30). But sometimes it is explicitly not related in this way (e.g. Job 2:3–7; Luke 13:1–5; John 9:2–3). However, the fact that sickness and death exist in the world at all is a result of sin entering the world.

It's well known that in London you are never far from a rodent. Recently I (Tim) came home to find droppings on the kitchen floor. My recent food hygiene training at church helped me discern that this was not ideal, and so I . . . swept up the droppings? Well yes, I did, but not only that. Cleaning up mouse droppings daily is of limited use. I also visited the local hardware shop and bought four peanut-butter-baited mouse-traps to deal with the root cause. Goodbye, Mickey.

In the Garden of Eden, before Adam and Eve ate the forbidden fruit, no-one got ill. There were no wheelchairs or cancer wards or get-well-soon cards. But then the world went horribly wrong. Jesus could just have swept up the droppings – a leper healed here, a paralytic raised up there. But when he makes the leper 'clean', and forgives the paralytic's sins, he is saying that he has come to deal not only with the symptoms of a broken world, but also with the thing that broke it in the first place. He has come to deal with sin.

In God's kingdom there is no place for sin.

Repent and believe in the gospel

Let's return to the 'A' bookends. It seems clear that the responses of Simon and Andrew, James and John are intended as a model for us. Jesus commands them: 'Follow me', and that's exactly what they do, even leaving behind their livelihood (1:18) and their family (1:20). Perhaps their response seems a little extreme?

A chapter later we come to Levi, and the command is the same: 'Follow me' (2:14). He leaves behind his lucrative career in the Inland Revenue and begins life as a disciple. But by this point in the narrative, given all that we've seen between the bookends, his response doesn't seem extreme at all.

Who wouldn't leave behind worldly gains for a kingdom in which there is no evil, no sickness, no sin? Who wouldn't choose to follow a King in whom is found not only authority, but also compassion, who stretches out his hand and says to a leper, 'I will; be clean'? If the kingdom is *this good*, and we know that not only 'from the catalogue', but also from the first-hand eyewitness testimonies of those who were in Capernaum to see it, who wouldn't want to respond in the way that Jesus has demanded?

> [T]he kingdom of God is at hand; repent and believe in the gospel. (1:15)

The Pharisee-o-meter (2:1 – 3:35)

I (Andrew) never understood the expression: 'missing the wood for the trees' as a youngster, basically because trees are made *out of* wood. But I think it's supposed to mean 'wood' as in 'forest'. The idea is that it's possible to focus so much on individual trees (an oak, a sycamore, a hornbeam) that you fail to see the bigger reality ('I'm in the Forest of Dean'). Probably this was obvious to you already.

Missing the wood for the trees is a common mistake when it comes to reading the Bible. You know that you've succumbed to this error if a chapter of the Bible becomes, for you, a series of entirely disconnected lessons: 'Jesus forgives sins; it's good to show hospitality to people different from you; fasting isn't always appropriate.' Instead, we should be looking for the overall message, the author's purpose, the 'forest'.

Your task is to look at the individual trees of 2:1 – 3:6 and to try to find out what kind of forest Mark has put us in. (We've already discussed the first two episodes under the heading of Jesus' kingdom, but there seems to be an overlap in Mark's structure, so that they also introduce a new theme that continues through this next section.)

DIG DEEPER: **Author's Purpose tool**

Read 2:1 – 3:6. Mark records five episodes ('trees') one after the other. Do they have anything in common?
Can you find any progression as we move through them?
Can you identify Mark's purpose (the 'forest')?

'We will not have you as our King' (2:1 – 3:6)

The scribes and Pharisees are archetypal baddies, up there with the man with the white cat and the swivel chair in Bond films. If we were to make a film of Mark's Gospel, we'd dress them in sinister outfits and choose as their theme tune the second movement of Shostakovich's 10th Symphony (find it on Spotify). But what if we try to give them the benefit of the doubt, at least at the beginning? In the spirit of British justice, let's treat them as innocent until proven guilty, and listen to Mark as the prosecuting barrister.

We first meet the scribes in the house with the gaping hole in the roof, questioning in their hearts how Jesus could dare to pronounce a man's sins forgiven. 'He is blaspheming!' they think to themselves (2:7). And . . . they have a point. Imagine that Tim has a bad conscience because of the dodgy tackle that left Rob with a broken leg. Andrew says, 'It's OK, Tim. I forgive you.' Rob thinks, 'Excuse me?!' Forgiveness is the prerogative of the one wronged, and because all sin is ultimately against God, only he can pardon it. The Pharisees are right to be a little shocked. That is, until Jesus perceives their unspoken thoughts (which is miraculous in itself) and offers physical proof that he is the Son of Man, endued with all God's authority to forgive. Now their private misgivings ought to give way to praise.

But they don't. Misgivings continue, this time over the company that Jesus keeps: 'Why does he eat with tax collectors and sinners?' (2:16). Again, they have a point. Imagine it was discovered that a well-respected member of your church spent his Friday evenings in the red-light district. You'd want to know why. 'I'm an AIDS worker,' he explains. 'Ah, fair enough, good on you,' you'd reply. Similarly, Jesus' explanation that he is a sin doctor ought both to reassure the scribes and to give them reason to admire him.

But it doesn't. Misgivings continue, this time over the impiety of Jesus' disciples: 'Why do John's disciples and the disciples of the Pharisees fast, but your disciples do not fast?' (2:18). Again, they have a point. Fasting in the Bible is frequently an expression of repentance or earnest seeking after God in a time of crisis. The fact that John (the Baptist)'s disciples are fasting underlines that it's not a bad thing to do. So why don't Jesus' disciples do it?

This is a great moment to pause and consider the difference that the **Author's Purpose tool** makes. If we were to treat these verses in isolation (as an individual tree), they would form the basis for a 'Should-Christians-fast?' sermon, and we would go off on a tangent, thinking about how and when we should fast. But, by now, we know that Mark's bigger point has nothing at all to do with fasting. That's just the presenting issue.

For the third time, Jesus' response to his critics centres on his *identity*. He was first the Son of Man, then the sin doctor, now the bridegroom. 'And fasting isn't really appropriate at a wedding reception, is it?' he asks. Jesus is alluding to Old Testament imagery that describes God as a husband to his people (e.g. Isaiah 62:5; Hosea 2:16). The Pharisees ought to recognize this claim to divinity and bow down to worship.

But they don't.

Imagine that you have a 'Pharisee-o-meter', with an arrow representing your assessment of the scribes' attitude on a scale that ranges from 'reasonable' to 'pig-headed' to 'psychopathic'. (Andrew has a cardboard version in his visual aid box.) Our guess is that, as you move through the episodes, the arrow swings further and further to the right. We're beginning to lose patience with them. It was fair enough to quibble at the beginning, when they might not have been quite sure who Jesus was. But now, as Jesus is about to warn them, they are heading into danger.

The quickest way to the heart of what Jesus is saying about garments and wineskins (2:21–22) is to focus on what they have in common. In both illustrations there is something new that doesn't fit with something old. This is a picture of the radical newness of Jesus' ministry clashing with the Pharisee's established traditions and expectations.[1] The other thing that is repeated is the outcome: 'the patch tears away'; 'the wine will burst the skins'; 'the wine is destroyed, and so are the skins'. To fail to make room for the new will lead to disaster.

But the Pharisees don't heed the warning; they plough on regardless. Or they are annoyed that the disciples plough on (excuse the pun). But, actually, the disciples don't plough or reap, both of which would have been classified as work and therefore transgressions of the fourth commandment (Exodus 20:8–11). They just snack. The Pharisees' objection seems nit-picking, to say the least.

Incidentally, we don't think that Jesus' disciples are breaking the law, nor that Jesus is setting aside the law – only that the Pharisees are misinterpreting it. We came to our view because of the following:

- Jesus' comment that 'the Sabbath was made for man,
  not man for the Sabbath' makes a point about the *original*

intention of the law. Jesus is not claiming to be changing anything. The Sabbath was always supposed to be a joy, not a straitjacket.

- There is nothing in the Old Testament to specify that 'plucking heads of grain' counts as work.
- Later in Mark (**Context tool**), Jesus will be fiercely critical of the extra stipulations and traditions that the rabbis added, while at the same time upholding the Ten Commandments themselves (7:1–13).

But we mustn't get distracted. Mark's main purpose isn't to focus on the Sabbath, but on the one who is 'Lord of the Sabbath'. Once again, he is making a point about Jesus' identity. That is why the illustration of David is so brilliantly chosen. Eating the temple bread while hungry might well have been 'not lawful' according to a Pharisee-type interpretation, but no Pharisee would have questioned David's actions, for the simple reason that . . . he was David! But for Jesus to do the same? It would be like walking on the grass at Buckingham Palace and, when questioned as to what on earth you think you're doing, answering, 'Didn't you know that the Queen walks on the grass?' The Queen does it, and so do I. David does it, and so do I.

Is this just a power thing, then? Might is right? I'm the King, so I'm above the law? No. Rather, Jesus is saying, 'I'm the King; I can *interpret* the law. And if the law for you means something that forbids snacking in a cornfield or would have let David starve, then you've got it wrong.' The Pharisees ought to abandon their traditions and acknowledge Jesus as the law's true interpreter.

But they don't. And in this final episode, Mark exposes them utterly. The arrow on the Pharisee-o-meter reaches the limits of the scale. Mark makes his case in various ways, and we need a whole range of tools to see this.

The **Structure tool** alerts us to a change in the order of the episode. Previously (four times), it has gone like this:

- Jesus (or the disciples) does something controversial.
- The Pharisees object.
- Jesus answers their objection.

But now their objection comes before Jesus even does anything. They are interested in his miraculous ability to heal only 'so that they might accuse him' (3:2). They have already made up their minds.

The **Look Carefully at the Text tool** (OK, this isn't one of the tools in the official toolkit, but sometimes just reading carefully is all you need!) helps us to understand the double meaning in Jesus' question. It could mean: 'Is it lawful *for me* on the Sabbath to do good or do harm, to save life or to kill?' That is, surely it's better to heal this poor man than to leave him in his current state. But it could also mean: 'Is it lawful *for you* on the Sabbath . . . ?' That is, can you not see the massive hypocrisy of fussing over the fourth commandment when you want to break the sixth by murdering me (see 3:6)? Whereas Jesus has been willing to answer every question put to him, their silence speaks volumes.

The **Tone and Feel tool** helps us to pause on v. 5: Jesus 'looked around at them with anger, grieved . . .'. The Pharisees' indifference to the man's suffering is just *wrong*. Jesus is *upset*. It's more than an exercise in theological point-scoring. It's personal.

The **Quotation/Allusion tool** helps us to understand the reference to their 'hardness of heart'. It's a phrase that harks back to Exodus (if you've read *Dig Even Deeper*, then you'll know about this), where it is synonymous with seeing huge amounts of evidence of God's power at work and choosing to ignore it all. How fitting.

The **Context tool** helps us to read the Pharisees' plot 'to destroy him' (v. 6) in the light of Jesus' earlier warning: 'The wine is destroyed, and so are the skins' (2:22). Heedless of the danger to themselves, they continue. Like a runaway train, there is no stopping them; a terrible crash is now inevitable.

Having worked hard at the text, let's now stand back and try to answer the question with which we began. What kind of forest has Mark put us in? What is his purpose? Surely it is to expose the Pharisees for the villains that they are. While there is a secondary application to how we view the Richard Dawkinses and Christopher Hitchenses of our own day, first and foremost, Mark is telling us something specific about those who opposed Jesus in the first century. If we think about it for a minute, that is actually more powerful. Those who were *actually there* (and therefore much better placed to reach an informed verdict than an atheist in Oxford 2,000 years later) did not reject Jesus because of a lack of evidence. Rather, they rejected him in the face of overwhelming evidence. Indeed, the very trap they set for Jesus depended on his ability to do the miraculous. They didn't doubt that he possessed such power. They just weren't willing to accept him as their King.

'I will not have you in my kingdom' (3:7–35)

If you take a text out of context, you're left with a con. That is the annoying-yet-memorable motto of the **Context tool**, and we need it here. We won't make sense of 3:7–35 unless we keep in mind that it follows 3:6; the purpose of the section is to show how Jesus responds to those who plot to kill him.

DIG DEEPER: **Context tool**

What difference does 3:6 make to your reading of each of the following sections?

- 3:7–12
- 3:13–19
- 3:20–21, 31–35
- 3:22–30

The first thing Mark records after the murder pact is Jesus' ministry of healing and exorcism by the sea. It's very similar to what has gone before (e.g. 1:32–34), and perhaps that's the whole point. Jesus carries on with business as usual. 'You want to kill me?' he seems to say. 'Don't think for a moment that that is going to hinder my mission.' And notice that the crowds think much more highly of him than the Pharisees and Herodians do. If anything, Mark stresses that Jesus is even *more* popular than before. People are coming from far-flung regions, as a few moments with 3:7–8 and a Bible atlas will reveal.

Then we hear about Jesus appointing twelve apostles in order that his ministry might expand – they too will preach and drive out demons. But is there even more going on? As we dig deeper, we need to observe closely the way in which Mark records things and the little clues that he gives as to their significance. Armed with the **Repetition tool**, for example, we couldn't help noticing this:

[H]e appointed twelve . . .
(v. 14)

He appointed the twelve . . .
(v. 16)

That's odd. Why tell us twice? Mark clearly wants us to notice the *number* of apostles. Twelve makes us think perhaps of the twelve patriarchs, the fathers of the twelve tribes of Israel. But why? In what way are the apostles like the patriarchs? Not everything that you notice in the text will be immediately clear, so for now let's note it in the margin as 'AFL' – awaiting further light.

Next, we read about Jesus' family (vv. 20–21), then about Beelzebul (v. 22–30), then about the family again (vv. 31–35). The **Structure tool** will have something to say about these together in a minute, but let's think about the Beelzebul bit first. The accusation that the scribes throw at Jesus reads as a desperate last resort. Unable to deny that he wields supernatural power over evil, and unwilling to acknowledge that this power comes from God, they go for the only remaining option: 'by the prince of demons he casts out the demons' (v. 22). Unfortunately, they didn't bother to check the logical coherence of their argument before opening their mouths.

Jesus' answer comes in three parts. First, in vv. 23–26, it's absurd to suggest that Satan casts out Satan. It would be like Britain declaring war on Britain. Or trying to sue yourself in court. To divide against yourself would be, to quote Blackadder, the worst way to fight a war 'since Olaf the Hairy, High Chief of all the Vikings, accidentally ordered 80,000 battle helmets with the horns on the inside'.[2]

Secondly, if it is not Satan who is behind the exorcisms, then it must be someone even stronger (v. 27). Jesus' exorcisms are evidence that he has bound the strong man and is plundering his house.

Thirdly, in vv. 28–30, those who oppose Jesus have placed themselves in enormous danger: 'whoever blasphemes against the Holy Spirit never has forgiveness.' This often scares Christians, because we wonder if we've done it. But before we apply it to ourselves too hurriedly, we need to look at what's actually being said:

- The **Linking Words tool** highlights v. 30 as the explanation for v. 29 (see the 'for'). Jesus warns them against blaspheming the *Holy* Spirit in response to their accusation that he has an *unclean* spirit. This is nothing less than calling good evil, naming God as Satan.
- The **Context tool** reminds us that Jesus warning them of blasphemy is the end point in a progressively worsening relationship that began with them accusing Jesus of blasphemy in 2:7. This is not an accidental slip of the tongue by someone first considering Jesus. Rather, it is stubborn, settled rejection by a group of people who have refused many opportunities to repent.
- The **Context tool** also gives us an insight into why this should be unforgiveable. If Jesus is the one who brings forgiveness through washing with the Holy Spirit (1:8 together with 1:4), then what forgiveness can there be for those who ultimately reject him?

It's right that these verses are very scary, but the true Christian has no need to be scared of them. It is those who persist in embittered opposition to Jesus who have cause to be alarmed.

Now it's time for the **Structure tool**. Is there any significance in the fact that the Beelzebul verses come *in between* the two mentions of his family? As we work through the rest of Mark, we'll discover that he's rather fond of this kind of 'sandwich' pattern, and in each case he uses it to demonstrate a connection between the bread and the filling. The filling here is about rejection of Jesus, as we've seen. And it turns out that the bread is about rejection too, but from a most unexpected source. What we read in 3:20–21 is a real shock if your view of Mary is shaped by Roman Catholic theology. Rather than doting beneficently on her Messiah Son, she is ready to have him sectioned: 'He is out of his mind.' By sandwiching this together with the scribes' blasphemy, Mark makes us very uncomfortable. Super-baddies are easy to write off, because none of our friends has (probably) ever gone so far as to call Jesus the devil. But Jesus' mother and brothers are altogether more ordinary, more likeable. They make no charges of demon possession. They simply think that Jesus has gone too far. And yet Mark lumps them together. Rejecting Jesus gently and respectably is rejecting Jesus just the same.

Jesus' response to the news that his family is waiting for him outside is startling (vv. 31–35). He ignores their summons, turns to the strangers sitting around him, and declares that *they* are his mother and brothers. Those who reject him are replaced.

At last we have the 'L' that we need for our 'AFL' above. As the Pharisees and Herodians reject Jesus, he turns to a collection of nobodies – some of them mere fishermen – and appoints *them* as Israel's new leadership (the equivalent of the twelve patriarchs). It's exactly the same idea: those who reject him are replaced.

In summary, then, how does Jesus respond to the rejection of 3:6 (and v. 21 and v. 22)? He rejects the rejecters. 'We will not have you as our King,' they complain, imagining perhaps that he needed their votes. 'That's OK,' he replies. 'I will not have you in my kingdom.'

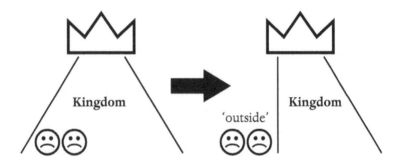

Tim is a glass-half-full person. Although he acknowledges that this is a chapter mainly about judgment, he doesn't want us to miss the amazing positive in v. 35. If we do the will of God – that is to say, if we honour his Son Jesus – we can be children of God. Now that's pretty amazing.

A sower went out to sow (4:1–34)

The purpose of parables

What are parables for? Think back to RE lessons at school, or perhaps to Sunday school. (Your parents may even have kept your felt-tip drawing of a farmer sowing his seed in their embarrassing-moments-from-your-childhood archive.) You were probably told something like this: parables are stories that Jesus told to make it easy for people to understand the truth about God.

Really?

What would 4:3–8 tell you about God, if this were the only bit of Jesus' teaching you heard? Answer: absolutely nothing. You'd conclude that as well as preaching the kingdom and casting out demons, Jesus had begun a sideline in agricultural education. The only thing that this parable tells you about is farming. Yes, of course, there is a profound spiritual meaning, but we know that only because we have read the explanation that was later given to a privileged few (vv. 13–20). To the 'very large crowd' (v. 1) who first heard him, and who lacked this explanation, his point was completely obscure.

What are parables for? Let's use some tools to think again.

DIG DEEPER: **Linking Words tool**

Read 4:10–12. How is the quotation from Isaiah connected to Jesus' decision to use parables?
Does this surprise you?

It's normally our policy not to give you the answers to the Dig Deeper exercises. But people struggle with this one – not because it's hard to understand what it says, but because we don't *want* it to say what it says. It's tempting to force the text out of shape and into a more palatable interpretation, or perhaps to reach for that most popular (but illegitimate) item in the toolkit, the **Skipping Over tool**!

What are parables for? To prevent outsiders from understanding the truth, so that they won't repent, so that they won't be forgiven. *That is what the text says.* We must be prepared to sit under the authority of God's Word when it says the hard things, even if that means a radical and sometimes painful shift in mindset. It would be great to pray that the same Holy Spirit who inspired these words would also help us to accept them.

Two further tools will help us to get our heads around this, and may soften the blow. First, the **Context tool**. In vv. 10–12, Jesus delineates two groups: 'those around him with the twelve', to whom the secret of the kingdom (and the explanation of the parable) is given, and 'those outside', who are kept from understanding. We've actually seen both groups before:

And his mother and his brothers came, and standing *outside* they sent to him and called him. And a crowd was sitting *around him*,

and they said to him, 'Your mother and your brothers are *outside*,
seeking you.' And he answered them, 'Who are my mother and
my brothers?' And looking about at those who sat *around him*,
he said, 'Here are my mother and my brothers!'
(3:31–34, italics added)

The context shows us that Jesus' decision to hide his saving
message in farming stories comes in response to people
rejecting him. It is to the people who said, 'We will not have
you as our King', that Jesus replies, in effect, 'In that case, I
won't let you understand my teaching.'

We get to the same answer using the **Quotation/Allusion
tool**. You've already looked at how the Isaiah quote fits into
Mark's narrative, but we can gain even more insight if we look
up its original context. God's decision to blind and deafen in
judgment (Isaiah 6:9–10) comes only after five chapters describing a people who refuse to turn to him. Indeed, among the
many woes that he pronounces, we find:

> Woe to those who call evil good
>   and good evil,
> who put darkness for light
>   and light for darkness,
> who put bitter for sweet
>   and sweet for bitter!
> (Isaiah 5:20)

We can't help thinking of the scribes in Mark 3 who blaspheme
the Holy Spirit by calling him an evil spirit. God hides his good
news in obscurity only in response to stubborn rejection. A
brief survey of Jesus' use of parables in Mark's Gospel confirms
this: it is a form of teaching reserved for when enemies are
around (3:23–27; 4:34; 7:14–17; 12:1–12).

Listen

If Jesus' use of parables highlights *his* initiative in deciding who can understand and who is left in confusion, then other aspects of the passage emphasize the part that we play in determining which of those groups we fall into. On the one hand, Jesus' disciples are those to whom he has 'given' the secret (4:11). On the other hand, they are those who 'asked him about the parables' (v. 10). As often in Scripture, divine sovereignty and human responsibility sit side by side.[1]

What is our responsibility? How do we avoid God's Word becoming parable-nonsense to us? A moment with the **Repetition tool** reveals a huge number of references to listening and hearing and ears (although the one in v. 28 does *not* count!). Our friend Dave decided to illustrate this for his Bible study group with a pair of inflatable ears, made from bicycle inner tubes, curled up inside a pair of tights, that he attached to his head. At every mention of a phrase related to hearing, he would pump more air into the tyres, so that by the end of the evening, his ears had grown to bicycle-wheel size. Yes, Dave is a little crazy!

The **'So What?' tool** is also relevant here, because several of the repeated ear-related phrases are direct imperatives (the circular 'signs giving orders' in our earlier road-sign analogy), and seem to capture Mark's purpose for his readers:

- Listen! (v. 3)
- He who has ears to hear, let him hear (v. 9).
- If anyone has ears to hear, let him hear (v. 23).
- Pay attention to what you hear (v. 24).

Mark wants to underline our responsibility to listen carefully to the Word of God. Having noticed that, we are better placed to understand some of the details of the passage, as they flesh out for us what listening will mean.

First, listening only counts if we keep listening. In the parable of the sower, the farmer's seed is variously munched by magpies, scorched by sunshine and throttled by thistles. Only some of it goes on to produce a viable crop. Jesus explains to his disciples that the seed represents the Word (v. 14), and each type of ground corresponds to a different group of people who 'hear the word' (vv. 15, 16, 18, 20). That is important. This is not a parable about some who hear and some who don't. Rather, it is about some who hear but Satan snatches the Word away; others who hear but lack sufficient roots to withstand religious persecution when it comes along; others who hear but get caught up with 'the cares of the world and the deceitfulness of riches and the desires for other things'. It is not enough to hear. Listening only counts if we keep listening.

This passage is, of course, an absolute gift to preach on at a summer camp. Tim remembers showering his teenage audience with porridge oats, these being the closest thing he could find to seed. Andrew took things a step further and cast an industrial hoover and a blowtorch in the roles of birds and sun respectively. It was fun to illustrate, but actually rather sobering at the same time. For even as Andrew was vacuuming up seeds, Satan was taking the gospel message away from some of the teenagers who were watching, so that by the end of the week they could remember almost nothing of what they had heard about Jesus. Just as Andrew toasted other seeds in the flame, so friends back at school were ready to taunt and bully the young Christian for her newfound faith to the point where she would give up. Even as Tim was holding up the biggest thistle he'd managed to find on the campsite, so the non-Christian girlfriend back home, the greasy pole of career advancement, the lie that money makes you happy, were ready to get a stranglehold on young Christian lives.

Wherever the Word is sown – at camp, in church, as you read this book – a fruitful outcome is far from certain. Listening only counts if we keep listening.

Secondly, listening should be expectant. Jesus' illustration that lamps are supposed to be seen (hence putting them on stands and not under bowls) is easily misunderstood here, because we are influenced by the explanation in the Sermon on the Mount – 'let your light shine before others' (Matthew 5:16). But like all itinerant preachers, Jesus sometimes used his favourite visual aids to illustrate different things at different times. How can we discover the meaning of lamps on stands *in Mark*? The **Linking Words tool** draws our attention to the very next verse: 'For . . .', and then we get our Mark-specific explanation: '. . . nothing is hidden except to be made manifest; nor is anything secret except to come to light' (4:22). Then the **Context tool** takes us back to v. 11 where the 'secret' in question was the meaning of the parables. Putting it all together, Jesus is saying that the parables are not supposed to keep everyone in the dark permanently. While the parables befuddle the outsider, Jesus always intended that the light of understanding would shine into the hearts of those who listened. Every time we open our Bibles, we can be confident that Jesus *wants* us to understand. So listening should be expectant.

Thirdly, listening must be active. Jesus expands on his 'if-anyone-has ears-to-hear-let-him-hear' refrain by talking about the 'measure you use' (v. 24). There are different amounts of listening. This presumably isn't referring to the number of verses you cover (as if reading Deuteronomy would earn you more points than reading 2 John) or the length of rambling sermon that you can manage to sit through. Rather, Jesus is pointing to the seriousness with which we take his teaching. If we come with a big measure, then 'more will be added' and 'more will be given'. But to the person who fails to listen, Jesus warns that 'even what he has will be taken away' (v. 25).

This is a great motivation to read our Bibles regularly, to open them longing to hear God speak. Shall we allow his truth to shape our thinking, even when it clashes with our culture? Or our own feelings? Jesus urges the Christian to keep listening.

But also, because the exhortation is for 'anyone who has ears to hear', it applies equally to the interested non-Christian. I (Andrew) only recently realized Mark's genius as an evangelist as I sat down in a coffee shop with a friend week by week to read through the Gospel and discuss it. First, Mark had shown my friend that Jesus was God's King, authenticated by the miracles that he performed in front of eyewitnesses. Then Mark had discredited Jesus' opponents, warning my friend not to respond with hard-heartedness as they had done. And then Mark told my friend to listen. I would never have devised an evangelistic course with 'Listen' as week three, but it came at just the right point – before Jesus said some of the things that my friend would find hardest to stomach, about sin and sex and hell. 'Stick with it,' Mark said. 'Keep listening.'

A bumper crop

Usually it's best to work through a Bible text in blocks of verses, so that a preacher might say, 'My first point is from vv. 1 to 4', and then 'my second point is from vv. 5 to 8', and so on. But Mark doesn't always write like that. Instead, he weaves different strands through the narrative. We've looked at the 'purpose-of-parables' strand, and the 'listen' strand. There's one more to consider.

In every one of the seed parables, things start small, but come harvest time, there is a bumper crop. In the parable of the sower, three-quarters of the seed sown yielded nothing. Unhappy farmer? No, because 'other seeds fell into good soil and produced grain, growing up and increasing and yielding thirtyfold and sixtyfold and a hundredfold' (v. 8). Even allowing for the lost seed, it's a huge return.

In the parable of the lazy farmer – not its official name, but the point seems to be that he does diddly-squat other than throw a bit of seed on the ground – 'The earth produces by itself, first the blade, then the ear, then the full grain in the ear' (v. 28). The emphasis is on the power of the Word to work without human intervention, as Martin Luther (the sixteenth-century monk whose gospel preaching changed the course of European history) testified:

> We should preach the Word, but the results must be left solely to God's good pleasure . . . I opposed indulgences and all the papists, but never with force. I simply taught, preached, and wrote God's Word; otherwise I did nothing. And while I slept, or drank Wittenberg beer with my friends Philip and Amsdorf, the Word so greatly weakened the papacy that no prince or emperor ever inflicted such losses upon it. I did nothing; the Word did everything.[2]

In the parable of the mustard seed, the emphasis is once again on small beginnings and a disproportionate outcome. A grain of mustard is tiny, and yet 'when it is sown it grows up and becomes larger than all the garden plants' (vv. 31–32). We tried to illustrate this by holding a mustard-seed-growing competition, although there were allegations of foul play when it became apparent that the clear winner, by several centimetres, was Odile, our resident Kew Gardens botanist!

The **Quotation/Allusion tool** reveals an added dimension, because the image of a great tree with birds nesting in the branches (v. 32) was used to describe the powerful earthly kingdoms that God brought to an end (Ezekiel 31:6; Daniel 4:12). Although the church is insignificant in geopolitical terms – and perhaps none have felt this as strongly as a bunch of fishermen following a carpenter's son in a far-flung corner of the mighty Roman Empire – on the last day it will be Jesus, and not Caesar, who reigns eternally.

To sum up, then, in every one of the seed parables, things start small, but come harvest time, there will be a bumper crop. What a huge encouragement! Perhaps you have only one or two colleagues who share your faith in Christ, while everyone else scoffs. Or perhaps you're at a university where members of the Islamic society outnumber those in the Christian Union by a ratio of three to one. Or perhaps you're from a country where Christians make up a tiny proportion of the population. It's easy to get discouraged. But picture the last day, harvest time, when Jesus' kingdom is revealed. There will be gathered 'a great multitude that no one could number, from every nation, from all tribes and peoples and languages' (Revelation 7:9). In fact, we are already well on the way. Jesus started with twelve followers. The number of Christians worldwide now runs into hundreds of millions.

At the time of writing, my (Andrew's) friend no longer meets me in the coffee shop to read Mark. I'm sad about that, and praying he'll come back. But in other coffee shops there will be other Christians reading Mark's Gospel with their friends. And some of them will listen. And keep listening. And listen expect-antly. And listen actively. And as Jesus promised, they will 'bear fruit, thirtyfold and sixtyfold and a hundredfold' (4:20).

Scared? (4:35 – 6:6)

In desperate situations, Jesus is powerful to save

On the 6th March 1987 the Roll-on/Roll-off passenger and freight
ferry *Herald of Free Enterprise* under the command of Captain
David Lewry sailed from Number 12 berth in the inner harbour
at Zeebrugge at 18.05 G.M.T. The *Herald* was manned by a crew
of 80 hands all told and was laden with 81 cars, 47 freight vehicles
and three other vehicles. Approximately 459 passengers had
embarked for the voyage to Dover, which they expected to be
completed without incident in the prevailing good weather. There
was a light easterly breeze and very little sea or swell. The *Herald*
passed the outer mole at 18.24. She capsized about four minutes
later . . . Water rapidly filled the ship below the surface level with
the result that not less than 150 passengers and 38 members of the
crew lost their lives.[1]

Thus reads the formal court report. I (Andrew) was eleven
years old at the time, and remember it being all over the news:
the worst peacetime maritime disaster since the sinking of the
Titanic. The story of the *Herald* is of course not a fairy tale; it

really happened. Similarly, Mark 4:35–41 describes a real boat, with real people, facing real danger. The only difference is that the passengers on board Jesus' boat were spared because of an extraordinary (but real) miracle.

The calming of the storm is the first in a series of four episodes (**Structure tool**), with a lesson so straightforward that we managed to boil it down to eight words: in desperate situations, Jesus is powerful to save. Hmmm. So why doesn't Mark just use eight words? As you read through this section, you will have noticed that Mark gives us an unusual amount of detail. Elsewhere, he can summarize a whole day of healings in a single sentence, but here he slows right down. That is our cue to reach for the **Tone and Feel tool**. We need to pay attention not only to the point being made, but also *how* it is being made. What is gained by the extra words? How do Mark's vivid descriptions help to hammer the point home in such a way that it engages with our emotions as well as our intellect? Let's look at the episodes one by one.

The situation is desperate: a 'great windstorm', Mark calls it. Waves crash over the side of the boat; it begins to fill with water. The boat's passengers assume that they will die – 'we are perishing' – and we should remember that these are not landlubbers, but experienced fishermen.

Jesus is powerful to save. The text conveys Jesus' total control of the situation in a quite delightful way, as a quick game of 'Spot the odd one out' will demonstrate: windstorm, waves, perishing, cushion! In Rembrandt's famous depiction of this scene (search for it on Google images), we don't even notice Jesus at first, snuggled up in the stern as chaos rages all around him. Then Jesus wakes from his nap and rebukes the raging ocean in the manner that a dog trainer might address a Labrador puppy: 'Siiiiit'. And it sits. It is calm. In fact, there is a 'great calm', says Mark, matching the 'great windstorm' of a moment ago.

The situation is desperate: a man possessed by a whole legion of demons, bent on self-destruction, uncontrollable by the villagers. The **Repetition tool** helps us with the detail: the man met Jesus 'out of the tombs . . . He lived among the tombs . . . Night and day among the tombs' (5:2, 3, 5). Here is a man living under the shadow of death. And that's not the only thing Mark repeats: 'And no one could bind him anymore, not even with a chain, for he had often been bound with shackles and chains, but he wrenched the chains apart, and he broke the shackles in pieces. No one had the strength to subdue him' (vv. 3–4). What a terrifying figure he must have been. His strength was superhuman, demonic. You can imagine mothers pleading with their children to steer well clear of the graveyard. This man was beyond restraining; he was a danger both to himself and to others.

Jesus is powerful to save. The great showdown between Jesus and lots of demons isn't the closely matched battle that some pseudo-Christian sci-fi books might lead you to expect. It's a walkover. The demons foresee their impending defeat and immediately raise the white flag, pleading with Jesus for leniency. He 'gave them permission' (v. 13, language that underlines his absolute authority) to enter a herd of pigs, which dives off the cliff forthwith. Oink-splosh.

At this point, some people get hung up on why Jesus is kind to demons and mean to pigs, but it's a misuse of the **Author's Purpose tool** to force Mark to engage with a twenty-first-century animal rights agenda that would have been foreign to him. What is *Mark's reason* for recording the clifftop cascade? We turned to some commentaries for help. They suggested, variously, that Jesus sent the demons into the pigs:

- as a visual demonstration that the demons have left the man

- to reveal the horror of what the demons would have done to the man, given time
- to trick them into destroying themselves (they didn't anticipate the lemming-like twist in the tale)
- to get rid of unclean spirits and unclean animals in a double whammy
- to mimic Pharaoh's drowning in the Red Sea (a bit more tenuous, this one)
- to destroy the Roman legion's food supply in a Jewish patriotic gesture (more tenuous still!)
- to give the Sea of Galilee a meaty taste (OK, we made that one up!)

This is a good illustration of why you should never work from only one commentary.[2] Any one of these pig-drowning explanations might look convincing in isolation, but when you are faced with six options, you have to go back to the text. Which is right?

The **Context tool** helps, because immediately afterwards Mark focuses our attention back on the demon-possessed man, now wonderfully transformed. Everything that happened to the pigs was a by-product of what Jesus did for him. In desperate situations, Jesus is powerful to save – that seems to be the author's purpose. But remembering that we are meant to be using the **Tone and Feel tool**, let's consider the beautiful way in which Mark describes it:

> [P]eople came to see what it was that had happened. And they came to Jesus and saw the demon-possessed man, *the one who had had the legion*, sitting there, clothed and in his right mind . . .
> (vv. 14–15, italics added)

We love the words in italics. In some ways they are unnecessary: it could have been no other man, given the previous thirteen verses. But it's as if Mark is anticipating our disbelief – 'Yes really, yes him, the crazy man, the violently-cutting-himself man; he's perfectly well.'

One further contribution from the **Context tool**: when we read that no-one before Jesus had been able to 'bind' him (v. 3), we can't help thinking of 3:27. Jesus is stronger than Satan, and plunders his house.

The situation is desperate: a woman who has been suffering a haemorrhage for twelve years and whose medical condition is worsening. Jesus is powerful to save: she is healed instantly. We're not going to comment on the tone and feel of this particular episode, because that's over to you.

DIG DEEPER: **Tone and Feel tool** (in combination with the **Translations tool**)

Read 5:25–28. How do the details of Mark's narrative paint the desperation of the woman's situation?
Sometimes the original Greek will have nuances that can only be captured in a very literal translation (you can find a couple at www.Biblegateway.com). How does the narrative build suspense leading up to the encounter with Jesus?

> [A] certain woman, having an issue of blood twelve years, and many things having suffered under many physicians, and having spent all that she had, and having profited nothing, but rather having come to the worse, having heard about Jesus, having come in the multitude behind, she touched his garment . . .
> (vv. 25–27, Young's Literal Translation)

Read 5:29–34. How do the details of Mark's narrative paint Jesus' power to save?

The situation is desperate: a local synagogue ruler falls at Jesus' feet, pleading desperately for his 'little daughter' who is 'at the point of death'. Jesus goes with him, but en route runs into the woman with the haemorrhage. The effect of this on the narrative is to introduce an *agonizing* delay. Picture an ambulance driver on a 999 call, stopping off to make a lengthy phone call while the family of the heart attack victim are forced to wait in the back, and you get something of a feel for what it must have been like for Jairus to watch the protracted 'who touched me?' discussions. The delay proves fatal: 'Your daughter is dead. Why trouble the Teacher any further?' (v. 35). There have been overtones of death throughout the section: the danger of 'perishing' in the storm, the 'tombs' where the man made his home, the worsening medical condition of the woman. But here it's more than an overtone. A twelve-year-old girl is dead. Her heart has stopped. She lies cold. On arrival, Jesus encounters a scene of public grief as only a Middle Eastern culture can express it, familiar to anyone who has watched news reports from Syria or Iraq: 'a commotion, people weeping and wailing loudly' (v. 38).

Jesus is powerful to save. As with his cheeky nap on the cushion in the storm, his quiet composure while others panic is striking: 'Why are you making a commotion and weeping? The child is not dead but sleeping' (v. 39). They laugh, but to express contempt rather than amusement. 'There's a time for pious sentimentality, Jesus, but this isn't it – a man has just lost his daughter!' But Jesus raises her from death as easily as Jairus might have woken her on a school morning. Again, notice how the details contribute to the tone and feel: here is one of only three instances in the Gospel where we are given Jesus' words in his mother tongue (v. 41), underlining the tenderness of the encounter. And there's the throwaway line at the end of v. 43. A moment ago the girl was dead, but now she could do with a bowl of Cheerios. It's so matter of fact. Everything is back to normal.

Fear and faith

We've seen four times over that in desperate situations, Jesus is powerful to save. At this point, we might easily put our Bibles away and spend some time thinking about how this applies to our lives. Not so fast, says the **'So What?' tool**. Correct application is itself a matter of close Bible study, because Mark himself wants to guide us to the correct response.

In particular, there is a lot in this section about fear and faith: 'Why are you so afraid? Have you still no faith?' asks Jesus of the petrified fishermen (4:40); 'Do not fear, only believe,' says Jesus to the grieving father (5:36). So our first stab at Mark's intended application might go something like this: because Jesus is powerful to save in desperate situations, we need never be afraid if we trust him.

Imagine you are catching the ferry back from Belgium after a weekend full of *moules-frites* and waffles. The name of the ship is the *Herald of Free Enterprise*. As the water starts to pour through the windows, you realize you might die, and you're a little nervous, to say the least. But because you're a Christian, you are spared the utter terror that grips others on board. You believe in a Saviour who can even get you through death, if it comes to that.

Imagine you are in a hospital waiting room, where the only thing to read is a pile of *Country Life* magazines, and you've been through all of them twice. Your daughter has been in surgery for hours. As the doctor approaches with a grave expression on her face, you're a little nervous, to say the least. But because you're a Christian, you are spared the utter terror that grips others in the waiting room. You believe in a Saviour who can even get your daughter through death, if it has come to that.

Because Jesus is powerful to save in desperate situations, we need never be afraid if we trust him.

So far so good. But Mark has more to teach us if we are prepared to dig deeper. We quoted two of his fear-sayings above, but in total there are five. Given that there is a 'desperate-situation/Jesus-intervenes/everything-is-OK' structure to each episode, you might expect the fearing always to come during the desperate situation. Intriguingly, that isn't the case:

Before Jesus intervenes	After Jesus intervenes
Afraid of a raging storm (4:40)	Afraid despite a calmed sea (4:41)
Afraid that a little girl has died (5:36)	Afraid despite an exorcized man (5:15)
	Afraid despite a healed haemorrhage (5:33)

How do we account for people being afraid *after* Jesus' intervention? It seems bizarre. To be afraid when waves are crashing over the side of your fishing boat is fair enough. But when the sea is as flat as a millpond, and the sun comes out and you're not going to die? Why on earth would you be afraid then? Mark is taking the application in a direction we might not have expected: Jesus takes away their fear of drowning only to substitute it with a new fear, a fear of him!

This idea of fearing Jesus instead of fearing death is backed up by the **Quotation/Allusion tool**, for there is much in common between this episode and Jonah chapter 1. There too we find a story of a near-shipwreck in a terrible storm, with one passenger managing to remain asleep. There too the sailors are afraid of perishing in the storm, but more afraid after it has been miraculously stilled.[3] Why be afraid after everything is

OK? Jonah makes it explicit – the pagan sailors have come to fear the LORD. They witness an act of extraordinary power and realize that they are dealing with the Creator of heaven and earth. Surely, a glimmer of some similar realization underlies the disciples' bewildered cry in Mark 4:41.

Mark also makes a contrast between Jesus-fear and death-fear when he sandwiches together the episodes of the dead girl and the bleeding woman (**Structure tool**). Not only do their stories intersect chronologically, but Mark links them by noting that the girl's age matches the length of the woman's illness (both twelve years) and by calling both of them 'daughter'. What is the significance of the comparison? The woman is afraid after Jesus' intervention. She fears Jesus. This is a sign of faith (5:34). Jairus is afraid before Jesus' intervention. He fears death. This is the opposite of faith (5:36).

So let's try to nuance our application. Before, we had: 'we need never be afraid if we trust Jesus', but now it becomes something like: 'Jesus is bigger than the things you're afraid of. Trust and fear him instead.'

Fear is a given. By nature, as small human beings, there will be things that daunt and overwhelm us. Just saying to an anxious person, 'Stop being anxious' doesn't work. Mark wants us to fill up all of our fear-capacity with a big view of Jesus. If he is the one who daunts us and overwhelms us, then there won't be room for other anxieties.[4] Ironically, it's only as we begin to fear him that we shall really start to trust him.

Think back to your imagined ferry trip on board the *Herald*. A small Jesus could help the captain to steer skilfully, or help the coastguard to come speedily, but once the boat is under water, there's little he can do. The only Jesus who can help in the face of death is one big enough to be scary. And the facts of history, the events of Mark 4 – 5, tell us that this is exactly the kind of Jesus we are dealing with. He has a terrifying amount of power. Therefore he is the one person we can trust wholeheartedly, whatever the situation.

Tempting as it to move on, we've still only covered four mentions of fear. One remains, and it comes as even more of a surprise:

> And they came to Jesus and saw the demon-possessed man . . . clothed and in his right mind, and they were afraid. And those who had seen it described to them what had happened to the demon-possessed man and to the pigs. And they began to beg Jesus to depart from their region.
> (5:15–17)

Like the woman healed of her haemorrhage, the villagers witness the astonishing power of Jesus. Like the woman, they are afraid. But instead of responding with fearful trust, they respond with fearful rejection (see also 11:18). They were more at home with evil than with the one who has power over evil. It is possible to see Jesus at his most powerful, at his most God-like, and still to oppose him. Indeed, this is exactly what happens in Jesus' home town (6:1–6). The people of Nazareth witness his teaching and his mighty works,[5] but they take offence because he is just the local boy, the carpenter. In the face of the evidence, their unbelief is quite astonishing (v. 6).

Let's summarize where we've got to with the **'So What?' tool**. In desperate situations, Jesus is powerful to save, and so:

- We need never be afraid if we trust him.
- We ought not to fear death, but fearfully trust Jesus instead.
- Others (astonishingly) will respond in fear and unbelief.

In a section with so many different responses, let's close with the **Repetition tool** and the man who had had the legion. Whereas the demons 'begged' Jesus for leniency, and the townspeople 'begged' Jesus to depart out of fear, the man 'begged' that he be allowed to go with Jesus (5:18). Having seen Jesus' incredible, scary power in this chapter, our response should be similar: Jesus, you are utterly trustworthy. Please let me be counted among your followers.

A head on a platter (6:7–30)

Would you rather sit a three-hour essay-based exam or a half-hour multiple-choice test? You'd think it would be a no-brainer, but multiple-choice tests can be harder than you think. Especially when the examiners are sneaky enough to come up with a series of options that look equally true.

DIG DEEPER: **Author's Purpose tool**

Read 6:14–29. Which of the following statements best summarizes Mark's point here? (We'd suggest you spend a good forty-five minutes on this, because you will need to look closely at the text and weigh the arguments for and against each one.)

a) See from Herod's confusion about Jesus how a guilty conscience can blind someone to gospel realities.
b) Realize it's dangerous to make rash promises, especially after a few drinks.

c) Prepare yourself for Jesus' rejection, as you consider John's fate; he too will be plotted against, executed and buried in a tomb.

d) Understand that failure to repent early on can lead to total rejection in due course.

e) See John the Baptist as the fulfilment (again) of the Old Testament prophet Elijah: both were opposed by the evil wives of morally compromised kings.

f) Expect preachers of repentance to receive bad treatment.

g) Realize how wonderfully different Jesus' rule is, as you ponder the differences between King Herod's sordid banquet and the meal that King Jesus is about to host (see 6:31–44).

h) Be appalled at how Herod beheaded his wife Herodias because she wouldn't listen to his favourite preacher.

Rather than going out of our way to be sneaky for the sake of it, we designed the Dig Deeper exercise to reflect exactly the kind of decisions that are needed in real-life Bible study. Eliminating (h) is easy, because it arises from a complete misreading of the text. Choosing between the options (a) to (g) is much more difficult, because every one of these statements finds at least some support in what Mark says. Here the question is not so much what is right, but what is *central*? Or how might the various fragments fit together into a larger whole?

No doubt you found yourself reaching instinctively for various tools. For example, when evaluating (a), perhaps you used the **Linking Words tool**, noting the 'for' between v. 16 and v. 17. The **Quotation/Allusion tool** would have been indispensable for weighing (e), as you read up on the relevant Old Testament background (e.g. 1 Kings 19:2; 21:25). Both (c) and (g) would have required the **Context tool**, as you read more widely in Mark's Gospel.

We began (as nearly always) with the **Structure tool**. The section opens with the story of Jesus sending the twelve on a mission trip (vv. 7–13), then the Herod story (vv. 14–29), then a single verse that rounds off the mission-trip story (v. 30). Why doesn't Mark finish one story before starting the next? It's another one of his sandwiches, where he deliberately intersects two episodes to emphasize a connection between them. Finding this connection will be the key to the author's purpose.

In the bread of the sandwich, the apostles 'proclaimed that people should repent' (v. 12). In the filling, John lost his head for telling Herod to repent of his illicit relationship (v. 18). This is a repentance sandwich. Repentance is the issue.[1]

You must repent

In vv. 17–20, Herod is sitting firmly on the fence. On the one side, he 'sent and seized John and bound him in prison' (v. 17). On the other side, 'he feared John, knowing that he was a righteous and holy man, and he kept him safe' (v. 20). He refuses to give in to Herodias' murderous wishes – he likes John too much. But he refuses to give in to John's preaching – he likes Herodias too much.

Sitting on fences seems reasonable to us in enlightened twenty-first-century society. It's what we do best. We have less sympathy for a king who serves up a severed head between courses at his dinner party. But Mark's point is that the fence-sitting of v. 20 leads inevitably to the moral disaster of v. 27. Fans of the comedian Harry Hill know exactly how it works: 'I like John the Baptist. But I like my brother's wife. Which is better? There's only one way to find out. FIGHT!' He can't have both. One will win.

And, of course, Herodias wins. She resents John's preaching, but can find no opportunity to kill him until . . . a birthday party! How perfect! At once she sets about choreographing a titillating dance, with her own daughter in the starring role. If we needed any confirmation that Herodias is pulling all the strings, we get it when, in response to an offer of half of the kingdom, the girl rushes to check with Mummy what she should say. 'Ask for John's head, darling,' she replies, clasping her hands together in delight, 'his head!' Then, in a macabre end to the episode, the head gets passed back along the chain of causation: the executioner 'gave it to the girl, and the girl gave it to her mother' (v. 28).

But Mark's emphasis on the part played by Herodias must be read in the context of v. 18. Her murderous hatred of John comes about 'For [**Linking Words tool**] John had been saying to Herod, "It is not lawful for you to have your brother's wife."' Her opportunity for evil comes as a direct consequence of *his* failure to repent. If only Herod had got off the fence and ended the relationship, none of this would have happened.

The impossibility of sitting on fences comes out also in Mark's account of the apostles' mission (vv. 7–13, 30). The villagers had two options: either welcome the repentance-preaching apostles as houseguests for the duration of their visit (v. 10), or refuse to listen, and have dust kicked at them as a sign of judgment (v. 11). Jesus' instructions to the apostles on what to pack – no food, no money, no warm clothes – force the issue. If their message were not embraced to the extent that someone offered them a place at the dinner table and a bed for the night, then they had no choice but to move on.

As we come to apply this to ourselves, we need the '**Who Am I?**' tool. Either we step into the shoes of the preachers of repentance – namely the apostles and John the Baptist – or we imagine ourselves as the ones preached to – the villagers and Herod. If the former, then the lesson becomes something like: 'Expect opposition as you share your faith. Look what happened to John the Baptist! Evangelism is going to be tough' (see also 13:9–13). If the latter, then the lesson becomes: 'Stop sitting on the fence and repent.' Getting the 'Who am I?' question right makes a big difference to the application.

Mark's choice of language cautions us against identifying ourselves too quickly with the preachers in this case. Rather than calling them 'disciples', Mark chooses more specific terms: 'the twelve' (v. 7) and the 'apostles' (v. 30). The only other place where these titles occur together is in 3:13–19 (**Context tool**), where Jesus chose this group from a much wider band of followers to be his special representatives. We are not apostles. But as we read the New Testament, we, like the villagers of Galilee, become hearers of the apostolic message. We need to repent.

The **Context tool** further confirms that we're on the right track, because this matches the headline application for the whole book:

Now after John was arrested [an explicit link to 6:14–29], Jesus came into Galilee, proclaiming the gospel of God, and saying, 'The time is fulfilled, and the kingdom of God is at hand; repent and believe in the gospel.'

(1:14–15)

This chapter really gets under the skin. The thing is, we're happy to repent most of the time. There are all sorts of things we're prepared to give up for Jesus. But there are also the things we want to hold on to. We kid ourselves that these don't matter. It's just a small compromise, we think. And at that point we're potential Herods.

Really? I have no intention of beheading anyone. I like Jesus' message. I enjoy listening to him.

Ah yes, but this is Mark's exact point. Herod enjoyed listening to John too. He didn't plan at the start to serve up John's head on a platter. But the small seed of unrepentance grew into a monster that Herod could not control.

For Herod, it was a sinful relationship. In our pastoral experience, sinful relationships are the biggest single cause of people eventually turning their backs on Jesus . . .

Don't sit on the fence. Repent.

Unrepentance took Jesus to the cross

When using the **'Who Am I?'** tool, we concluded that we are to identify primarily with those preached to, rather than the preachers. Fair enough. But it seems that Mark is also using this account to tell us something specific about the suffering that awaits a particular preacher. As the **Context tool** reveals, John's fate closely parallels the fate of Jesus:[2]

Herodias wants John dead, but has to wait for the right opportunity (6:19, 21).	The chief priests and the scribes want Jesus dead, but have to wait for the right opportunity (14:1, 10–11).
Herod capitulates to peer pressure as he reluctantly gives the order for John's execution (6:26).	Pilate capitulates to peer pressure as he reluctantly gives the order for Jesus' execution (15:15).
John's disciples took his body and 'laid it in a tomb' (6:29).	Joseph of Arimathea took Jesus' body and 'laid him in a tomb' (15:46).

'You must repent,' said John. But Herod was unrepentant and turned violently against the Baptist. 'You must repent,' said Jesus. But humanity was unrepentant and turned violently against God's Son. Unrepentance took Jesus to the cross.

Bread of heaven (6:31–52)

Jesus fed 5,000 with five loaves

Feeding yourself out in the countryside without access to a supermarket is quite difficult. I (Tim) discovered this on an SAS Survival Guide-inspired holiday in Croatia with two friends. With a canoe as transport and hammocks for beds, we vowed to eat only what we could forage or catch.

On Day One, we were pretty optimistic. Having fashioned a harpoon out of bamboo, we paddled out to sea, taking turns to don the snorkel and hunt the passing shoals of sardines. Our fishing style involved lots of thrashing around and stabbing violently at shadows, so we quickly worked up a hearty appetite. Which was unfortunate, given that we caught . . . nothing. We did manage to scrape a few mussels off a jetty, but they didn't go far. You can imagine our feeling of dejection as we headed round the coast to the nearest tourist hotspot and joined the queue for pizza.

Compared with the situation described in Mark 6, the odds had been somewhat in our favour. There were only three of us, and (at least in theory) a whole sea of fish. Jesus was in the desert with only two fish, plus five loaves of bread, and more than 5,000 mouths to feed. But amazingly, 'they all ate and were satisfied. And they took up twelve baskets full of broken pieces and of the fish' as leftovers (vv. 42–43).

It's hard to get your head round the numbers at first. I (Andrew) tried to illustrate it on my summer camp by carting our entire bread supply – enough to feed 150 hungry teenagers and leaders for one day – from the kitchen to the stage. 'Imagine a tower of Hovis thirty-three times bigger than this,' I said. 'That's how much bread you would need to feed 5,000 people, *normally*. But Jesus managed it with a few bread rolls.' Then I tried to illustrate it the other way round. The equivalent to the amount of bread Jesus started with was one-seventh of a bread roll between the lot of us. So we shared this out row by row and then passed round baskets for the leftovers. Considering each person got less than a crumb, there wasn't much to collect.

Before we think about any spiritual lesson that Mark may have for us, we need to reach for the **Genre tool** and remind ourselves that this is historical narrative and not parable. Both kinds of literature can teach us true things, of course: we learned something from Jesus' story about a farmer sowing seed, even though that particular farmer didn't really exist and was just made up for illustration purposes.

But it's very important to realize that miracles are not just illustrations. They are eyewitnessed events. They really happened.[1]

Why does the genre matter though, if we learn the same spiritual truth either way? Simply because:

> 'It's a fact of history that Jesus
> miraculously multiplied bread   = Life-changing
> out of compassion.'

'It's nice to imagine a powerful, compassionate Jesus as pictured in this made-up story about a shared lunch.'	=	As limp as a lettuce that's been left in the sun for days

The greatest rescue operation in history is underway

Having stopped to appreciate this as a historical event, we can then (and only then) move on to think about what it might mean. At one level, it is simply one more piece of evidence that Jesus can do things no-one else can do. But digging deeper, we find that more is going on.

The clue comes right at the end of the passage: 'for they did not understand about the loaves, but their hearts were hardened' (v. 52). Stop reading this book and have a think about that verse for a minute, and see if you can do your own detective work before you read on.

OK, so this was our thought process. The sentence begins with a 'for', and so we used the **Linking Words tool** to think more carefully about the connection that Mark is making with what has gone before. The disciples are astonished that Jesus walked on water, *because of* their failure to understand the feeding of the 5,000. Right. So if they had understood the feeding, then somehow walking on water shouldn't have astonished them? Miraculous feeding and miraculous water-crossing must be connected somehow. That was step one.

Next, we had to work out how they are connected. Something to do with the book of Exodus? That's the obvious place where miraculous feeding (manna from heaven, Exodus 16) and miraculous water-crossing (the parting of the Red Sea, Exodus 14 – 15) come together. And so out with the **Quotation/Allusion tool** as we look for evidence that Mark really does have Exodus in mind.

Time for a little aside. People differ in the degree of caution that they exercise when using the **Quotation/Allusion tool**. At one extreme, there are those who see connections everywhere, so that it becomes an exercise in random word association (or a game of Mornington Crescent, if you're a Radio 4 listener!): 'He fed 5,000 with two fish, and in Jerusalem there is a gate called the Fish Gate, and so . . .' At the other end of the spectrum, there are those who bury their head in their hands at such allusion-mania. For them, nothing less than an 'it is written in Isaiah the prophet' will do.

How do we steer a course between these extremes, so that we pick up all of the allusions that Mark intended, without making spurious connections that aren't really there? In the original *Dig Deeper*, we explained the 'general rule of thumb . . . that the more specific or unusual the expression, the less likely it is that its use in two places in the Bible is coincidental' (p. 120). That means that unusual or technical words like 'Passover' count for more than common words like 'fish'. Also, a whole phrase like 'abomination that causes desolation' counts for more than 'abomination'. In addition, the boffins suggest that we should be more persuaded by:

- multiple allusions to the same Old Testament text
- allusions to two different texts that are themselves interconnected in some way
- allusions to a 'favourite' text – i.e. a part of the Bible to which Mark keeps returning

Let's use these criteria to find out whether Mark really is alluding to Exodus. We've mentioned already that both feature miraculous feedings. The connection is strengthened when we find that both feedings took place in the desert (not in the *dessert*, as Andrew first mistyped it, for then there would have been plenty of food already!). Mark underlines this by describing the terrain no fewer than three times (**Repetition tool**, vv. 31, 32, 35). Some also think that Jesus' glance towards heaven as he gives thanks (v. 41) echoes the heavenly origin of the manna in Exodus, and that the groups of fifty and a hundred in which people sit to eat hark back to the administrative units suggested by Moses' father-in-law, Jethro.

We also suggested that the walking on water relates to the Israelites' safe passage through the Red Sea. Again, various details fit nicely. In both cases, it happened during the night, shortly before dawn, and in both cases, it was unusually windy (one commentary even goes to the trouble of proving that the wind *direction* is a match).[2]

Add to all this that Jesus 'meant to pass by them' (v. 48), just as God passed by Moses hidden in a cleft in the rock, and that Jesus hiked up a mountain to speak with God (v. 46), as Moses was wont to do, and that Jesus borrowed from the burning bush script when he said, 'I AM' (v. 50, with help from the **Translations tool**), and that Mark describes in distinctively Pharaoh-like terms the disciples' failure to understand (v. 52). On the 'multiple-allusions-to-the-same-text' criterion, it's pretty convincing![3]

DIG DEEPER: **Quotation/Allusion tool**

So far, we have been pushing our Exodus theory. But it's possible that Mark 6 is consciously alluding to some other passages too.

Candidate 1
Read Ezekiel 34.
Mark 6.34 is the obvious point of contact. But in Ezekiel,

there are two kinds of shepherd. If Jesus fulfils the role of
one, is there anyone in the immediate context of Mark who
fits the description of the other? (Hint: the prophets use the
term 'shepherd' to refer to the kings of Israel.)
Are you persuaded that Mark intended to allude to Ezekiel?

Candidate 2
Read Isaiah 40.
Mark 6.34 also connects with Isaiah 40:11. But there may
be another link. Back in chapter 1, Mark repeated the word
'wilderness' three times in relation to a quote from Isaiah
40:3. Here he again uses the same word three times
(although, annoyingly, it gets camouflaged in some
translations as 'desolate place'). Is saying 'wilderness
wilderness wilderness' Mark's deliberate clue to an Isaiah
40 connection?
Are you persuaded that Mark intended to allude to Isaiah?

Candidate 3
Read 2 Kings 4:42–44.
How do the details of the account of Elisha's miracle line up
with Mark's report of the feeding of the 5,000? Does the fact
that Elisha was Elijah's successor suggest any further
connections (given the allusions to Elijah in Mark chapter 1)?
Are you persuaded that Mark intended to allude to 2 Kings 4?[4]

Can Mark really be alluding simultaneously to Exodus, Ezekiel,
Isaiah and 2 Kings? We noted above that we should be more
persuaded by 'allusions to two different texts that are themselves interconnected in some way'. And, as it happens, each
of the texts in the Dig Deeper box has its own links to Exodus,
as the following diagram attempts to show.

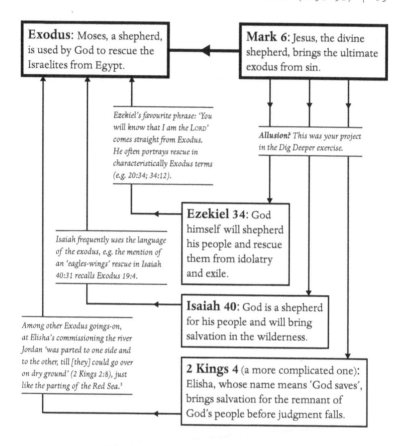

Exodus: Moses, a shepherd, is used by God to rescue the Israelites from Egypt.

Mark 6: Jesus, the divine shepherd, brings the ultimate exodus from sin.

Ezekiel's favourite phrase: 'You will know that I am the LORD' comes straight from Exodus. He often portrays rescue in characteristically Exodus terms (e.g. 20:34; 34:12).

Allusion? This was your project in the Dig Deeper exercise.

Ezekiel 34: God himself will shepherd his people and rescue them from idolatry and exile.

Isaiah frequently uses the language of the exodus, e.g. the mention of an 'eagles-wings' rescue in Isaiah 40:31 recalls Exodus 19:4.

Isaiah 40: God is a shepherd for his people and will bring salvation in the wilderness.

Among other Exodus goings-on, at Elisha's commissioning the river Jordan 'was parted to one side and to the other, till [they] could go over on dry ground' (2 Kings 2:8), just like the parting of the Red Sea.[5]

2 Kings 4 (a more complicated one): Elisha, whose name means 'God saves', brings salvation for the remnant of God's people before judgment falls.

It does kind of make your head explode. But this mass of inter-connections shouldn't really surprise us, because just as in the ancient world all roads led to Rome, in the Bible every road leads to Jesus, 'For all the promises of God find their Yes in him' (2 Corinthians 1:20).

By linking Jesus to the exodus, Mark is saying something breathtakingly significant. He is saying that Jesus has not come only to bring a series of mini-rescues – cleansing one leper, eating with one tax collector, raising one man's daughter – but *the* Rescue, with a capital R. The exodus was a decisive turning point in Israel's history. For hundreds of years, God's people looked back on it as the defining moment of salvation. And yet, towards the close of the Old Testament, some of the prophets (such as Isaiah and Ezekiel) started to speak in terms of another, even greater, exodus to come, when God himself would come as a Shepherd and rescue his people from sin.

So, as Jesus feeds a crowd with some bread, and crosses water on foot, Mark shouts at us, 'It's here. The moment that Isaiah and Ezekiel had been longing for. The new exodus has arrived!' And in the same breath he also shouts at us, 'He's here. The figure that Isaiah and Ezekiel had described with such awe and wonder. The divine Shepherd has come!'

Heart failure (6:53 – 7:23)

'You have defiled hands'

In 1952, a man named Geoffrey Handley-Taylor analysed a collection of 200 traditional nursery rhymes. You'd think, if anything would paint a rose-tinted picture of the world, it would be a nursery rhyme. But he found (among other things):

- eight allusions to murder (unclassified)
- two cases of choking to death
- one case of death by devouring
- one case of cutting a human being in half
- one case of death by squeezing
- one case of death by shrivelling
- one case of boiling to death
- four cases of killing domestic animals
- seven cases relating to the severing of limbs
- one case of the desire to have a limb severed
- eight cases of whipping and lashing
- fourteen cases of stealing and general dishonesty
- sixteen allusions to misery and sorrow
- four cases of cursing
- one allusion to marriage as a form of death
- nine cases of children being lost or abandoned

- two cases of house burning
- nine allusions to poverty and want
- two cases of unlawful imprisonment
- two cases of racial discrimination

Mr Handley-Taylor was scandalized that such 'unsavoury elements' should be found in literature designed for innocent children, and he joined others in calling for nursery rhyme reform. If we can limit children's exposure to corrupting influences, people thought, then they will grow up the better for it. It's the logic behind PG certificates on films, and child-friendly internet search engines. It makes total sense. And the Pharisees of Jesus' day would have said a loud 'Amen'.

The Pharisees, you see, were very concerned about what you allowed into your body from the outside. That's why they were strict about eating only kosher food. And they were scrupulously careful about washing their hands first. And washing the cups they drank from. And pots. And copper vessels. And dining couches (?!). Mark's decision to give quite so many examples suggests that he thought the Pharisees a little obsessive! But anyway, they wash everything, and Jesus doesn't, and so there is an argument.

Using the **Structure tool**, we can see that Jesus answers the Pharisees' objection in two stages.

'Why do your disciples not walk according to the tradition of the elders . . .' (7:5a)	Jesus responds in vv. 6–13
'. . . but eat with defiled hands?' (7:5b)	Jesus responds in vv. 14–23

'Traditions, shmaditions'

Jesus' opening gambit, using a quotation from the prophet Isaiah, is to denounce his opponents as hypocrites (vv. 6–8). Their piety is mere pretence. They are paying lip service to God while busying themselves with a religious system of their own making. The endless ceremonial washings are a sham.

Then Jesus shows exactly why Isaiah's mud sticks. Let's use the **Structure tool** again to see how the argument works:

> You're very adept at rejecting God's commandments in order to establish your traditions (v. 9).
>> And here's one damning example of how you do that (vv. 10–12).
> I'll say it again. You make void God's word by your traditions (v. 13a).
>> I've got plenty more examples if you'd care to argue . . . (v. 13b).

Jesus' damning example is the practice of 'Corban', a way of ring-fencing certain funds for religious use so that they couldn't be used to pay nursing home fees, for example. On the surface, it might have looked pious: 'Sorry Mum, but God is our number-one priority; I'm sure you understand.' In reality, it showed that they didn't care for God at all. Honouring your father and mother had come in at number five in God's top ten. It was so important that God had prescribed the death penalty for any Israelite who failed to keep this commandment. And yet the Pharisees were happy to set it aside in order to maintain their own man-made regulations.

It's always risky to apply a passage before you've understood it completely, and so we're not going to fire with both barrels of the **'So What?' tool** until we have considered part two of Jesus' answer (vv. 14–23). But we should at least expose our consciences to Jesus' implicit warning about money. Yes, it's just an example that helps to make a broader point. But, as we read through Mark, we'll find that money is the example surprisingly often.

'You have defiled hearts'

Jesus now turns to the second half of the Pharisees' question: 'Why do your disciples eat with defiled hands?' We could paraphrase his answer in v. 15 as follows: 'Defilement isn't outside in. It's inside out.'

According to the Pharisees, defilement was outside in. But with a very simple biology lesson, Jesus shows that eating unkosher food or eating with hands that have touched something 'unclean' cannot be the reason for inner defilement. 'Do you not see that whatever goes into a person from outside cannot defile him, since it enters not his heart but his stomach, and is expelled?' (vv. 18–19). Think back to the diagrams on your science classroom wall. One of them showed the digestive system, and went something like this: *fork ⇒ mouth ⇒ oesophagus ⇒ stomach ⇒ intestines ⇒ loo*. If in an exam you had written *fork ⇒ oesophagus ⇒ heart*, then you would have got an F. No cardiac surgeon has ever been asked to remove sweetcorn from a heart valve. Defilement isn't outside in.

A quick contribution from the **Vocabulary tool**: our Greek lexicon defines *kardia* (heart) as the 'centre and source of the whole inner life, with its thinking, feeling and volition'.[1] Elsewhere in Mark, it is the organ with which someone can question (2:6), doubt (11:23) and love God (12:30). In modern thought, we might associate these things with the brain, but Jesus' point would still stand: the brain isn't part of the digestive system either.

The thing is, problems that are 'outside in' are *fixable*. To borrow a slogan from a highbrow TV programme: 'Bob the builder, can we fix it? Bob the builder, yes we can!' We can check what goes in. We can restrict our diet. We can clean our dining couches. We can edit our nursery rhymes.

But Jesus says our problem isn't outside in. So where is it from? It's inside out. This is the message of vv. 20–23, although we often misread these verses. We tend to put the emphasis on the terrible things that we find in human nature:

> For from within, out of the heart of man, come *evil thoughts, sexual immorality, theft, murder, adultery, coveting, wickedness, deceit, sensuality, envy, slander, pride, foolishness.* All these evil things come from within, and they defile a person.
> (7:21–23, italics added)

But Jesus' new contribution is not to tell us that terrible character traits exist. That wasn't the point at issue. Even today's most vehemently anti-Christian social commentators wouldn't deny that people are murdered in Britain most days of the week, or that slander in the office is pretty common. Rather, Jesus is making a point about the source of such things. We should probably read the emphasis more like this:

> For *from within, out of the heart of man,* come evil thoughts, sexual immorality, theft, murder, adultery, coveting, wickedness, deceit, sensuality, envy, slander, pride, foolishness. All these evil things *come from within,* and they defile a person.

No-one needs to teach us to be corrupt. It's not as if a child is innocent until they read about Hansel and Gretel baking a witch in an oven. We are unclean already before we are negatively influenced. The problem is there already, on the inside.

Now is the time to give it both barrels with the **'So What?' tool**. Most religions (and even secular non-religion) are based on the Bob the Builder principle: sure, there's a problem, and it might take hundreds of Hail Marys, or a trip to Mecca, or a few cycles of reincarnation upwards, but we can fix it. It might take a year working for an NGO in the Third World, or radical commitment to green energy and recycling programmes, but we can fix it. This links back into the first half of the passage, because fixing the problem was what the Pharisees' ceremonial washings were about. It was what Corban was about. And far from yielding a solution, their man-made religion just made things worse. Throughout this chapter, Jesus sets about demolishing our Bob-the-Builder confidence. He says that we *can't* fix it.

Jesus wants us to realize that our moral failure is intrinsic to who we are, that when we want to point the finger of blame, we had better do so in front of a mirror, and that we can't fix it. There is evil inside of us. Our hearts are defiled.

As we were both mulling this over, we realized that we deny this almost every time we apologize to someone. We say, 'I'm sorry I did such and such, but . . .', and after the 'but' comes a mitigating circumstance, an explanation of why our actions were unavoidable really, a finger of blame pointed away from ourselves. Essentially: 'I'm sorry I did this, but in my defence it was outside in.' So, recently, we've tried making apologies in a way that takes Mark 7 seriously: 'I'm sorry I was late – I was selfishly caring more about my time than yours'; or 'I'm sorry I snapped at you – there was malice in my heart.' It sounds so stark to say that, such an admission of moral bankruptcy. It's really, really hard to apologize Mark 7 style.[2]

DIG DEEPER: **'So What?' tool**

We haven't finished the business of Bible study until our thinking has really changed and the connections inside our

head have been rewired. So this Dig Deeper exercise is a bit
more . . . practical than usual:
The next time you need to apologize, force yourself to do it
Mark 7 style.

Before we conclude, we have a caution regarding proper use
of the 'So What?' tool for the preachers among you: in our
desire to drive the point home, we mustn't get so carried away
that we say more than the Bible does. We should be preaching,
'Your hearts are the source of evil', but a flash of pulpit-
thumping rhetoric can easily turn this into: 'You're every bit
as evil as Hitler' or 'There's nothing good to say about you.'
This is where the discipline of systematic theology can provide
a useful check: at its best, systematic theology is just about
using the **Context tool** at the level of the whole Bible, making
sure that we do not 'so expound one place of Scripture, that
it be repugnant to another'.[3]

So, are we every bit as evil as Hitler? No, inasmuch as
God makes distinctions between different sins and the dif-
fering punishments they deserve (e.g. Exodus 21 – 23; Luke
12:47–48; Romans 2:6), and so he doesn't think that exter-
minating 6 million people and lying to your grandma
are morally equivalent. But the point of Mark 7 is that
we have the same fundamental heart condition as Hitler,
because his evil acts and my (lesser) evil acts have the same
source.

Is it true that there's nothing good that can be said about
us? No, inasmuch as we were created in God's image, with
great value and dignity (Genesis 1:26–27). We are not mere
bags of chemicals, as the materialist thinks. Yet this makes the
state of our hearts all the more tragic – we were intended to
be noble, but are now horribly corrupted.

Is it all bad news?

The message of this chapter hasn't been easy to accept. But it's not all bad news. Here are two glimmers of a silver lining to keep us from the brink of despair.

First, when we read that 'his disciples asked him about the parable' (v. 17), our ears pricked up, and out came the **Context tool**. We know from earlier in Mark that parables are for outsiders, but the explanation is given in private only to Jesus' trusted friends (see 4:11). Mark clearly therefore uses v. 17 to flag up teaching that is reserved for those close to Jesus. How striking! The truth about evil hearts is not for Jesus' enemies, but for his disciples. In the context, we should read it not as the condemning sentence of the judge, but as the loving diagnosis of the sin doctor (2:17).

Secondly, the concept of being 'defiled' is similar to the notion of being 'unclean' (although a different Greek word is used). In the very next episode, we are going to see how Jesus deals with a little girl possessed with an unclean spirit. Read on.

Crumbs for the dogs (7:24 – 8:10)

Neither of us handles awkwardness well. I (Andrew) still remember the family visit to a tearoom in the cathedral city of Ely – the kind of place with doilies on the plates and little pink flowers on the china – when someone at the table let out a deafening burp. My grandma didn't know where to look. The embarrassment was excruciating.

Sometimes we feel the same embarrassment at Jesus. He insists on saying things that we would rather he didn't say. Imagine the outrage in the frilly tearoom if someone had likened one of the waitresses to a dog! Many people rush to explain 7:27 away. Some point out that the Greek uses a diminutive form, so we should perhaps translate it 'little dog' or 'puppy'. Any offence that could have been implied is thereby mitigated with mental images of Labradors chasing toilet rolls, and we kid ourselves that Jesus is saying something equivalent to: 'You're cute.' Hardly. Others tell that this was a normal way for Jews to speak of Gentiles. Normal, perhaps. Inoffensive, no.

The fact is, Jesus didn't call the woman a 'dog' by mistake. He intended to say 'dog', and he knew full well how much it would have us squirming in our seats. And as long as we want to replace it with a word other than 'dog', we haven't grasped the point he is making.

Can dogs be saved?

Let's begin with the **Author's Purpose tool**. Mark is reporting an exorcism (7:24–30). He wants us to know that Jesus had compassion on a little girl and freed her from the grip of evil. But this is nothing new for his readers: we have seen many times that Jesus has authority over evil spirits (remember oink-splosh). As users of the **AP tool**, we are not satisfied. We want to ask, why has Mark included another exorcism *here*? How is he seeking to move our understanding on?

As we read and reread these verses, we find everywhere an emphasis on the woman's ethnicity. We learn in v. 24 that the disciples were passing through 'the region of Tyre and Sidon', which is across the border in non-Jewish territory.[1] But in case our geography isn't up to scratch, Mark underlines the point in v. 26 by telling us twice: she's a Gentile; she's a Syrophoenician! Readers, do you get me? She's not Jewish. Now the **AP tool** has got its teeth into something. Mark is exploring how Jesus' mission relates to Gentiles.

So what does Jesus say to a Gentile? We can summarize it in two brief statements: You're not entitled. But by grace you can be included.

The one thing more surprising than Jesus calling a woman a dog is her response. Instead of slapping him in the face and saying, 'How dare you!', her first words are: 'Yes, Lord' (v. 28). To our ears, this is extraordinary. How come she is not offended, while we are so offended on her behalf? The answer is that she doesn't share our twenty-first-century Western sense of entitlement. She doesn't stand on her rights. Indeed, she realizes she has no rights on which to stand. She knows that, as a non-Jew, she has no stake in the kingdom promised to God's 'children'. Yet, encouraged by Jesus' hint that there might be blessings to spare (with his comment that the children should be fed 'first'), she is content to assume the role of a dog scrounging under the table. She will be more than happy with the scraps.

The woman's response impresses Jesus: 'For this statement you may go your way; the demon has left your daughter' (v. 29). Although the woman is not entitled to a share in God's blessing, indeed *because she recognizes that she is not entitled*, she is included by grace. Shame on us if we are offended by being called a dog. Shame on us if we thought for a second that God owed us anything. Empty-handedness is always the starting point for grace.

> Nothing in my hand I bring,
> Simply to Thy cross I cling;
> Naked, come to Thee for dress;
> Helpless, look to Thee for grace;
> Foul, I to the fountain fly;
> Wash me, Saviour, or I die.[2]

Next up, Mark gives us a detailed description of a deaf man being healed. We challenge anyone to get 'Ephphatha' into a game of Boggle! With the **Context tool** in mind, we find ourselves asking what this has to do with the exorcism of a Gentile woman's daughter. Again, the geography provides a clue. We learn in v. 31 that Jesus has continued his journey through Gentile territory until he reaches the 'Sea of Galilee, in the region of the Decapolis'. The Decapolis was mentioned back in 5:20 in relation to an episode featuring pig farming, which for obvious reasons was not a priority among Jewish people. Perhaps we are to understand that this miracle too involves a Gentile?

The supper that gives you déjà vu

Next up, we get a description about Jesus feeding a large number of people with an in-normal-circumstances inadequate quantity of bread and fish. Hmmm. Is it just us, or is this sounding uncannily familiar – not just in what happens, but even in the way that the story is told? It seems that Mark is going out of his way to demonstrate the parallel with what has gone before.[3]

DIG DEEPER: **Context tool**

How many parallels can you find between the feeding of the 5,000 (6:30–44) and the feeding of the 4,000 (8:1–10)? Look out for places where Mark uses exactly the same words, or where he narrates certain features in exactly the same order.

Having noticed the similarities, we now need to reach for the **Author's Purpose tool**, and ask the question: 'Why?' Why do we need not one feeding, but two? There actually seem to be a couple of answers to this, one of which will have to wait until the next chapter. But for now, let's see if there is any mileage in following through the Gentile theme that has been so prominent in the context: in contrast to the 5,000 Jews who were fed back in chapter 6, perhaps the 4,000 are Gentiles?

Several pieces of evidence have been suggested in support of this. For example, there are seven baskets of leftovers (v. 8), in contrast to the twelve at the feeding of the 5,000; twelve is a distinctively Jewish number, and seven (we're told) represents completeness and therefore the inclusion of the Gentiles. Hmm. The problem is that proofs concerning numbers are too often in the eye of the beholder. Why hasn't anybody chosen to give us an explanation of the number five (loaves at the first feeding), or the number two (fish at the first feeding), or the number three (days that the crowd in 8:2 had not eaten)?! Another line of argument makes much of the different Greek words for 'basket' in 6:43 and 8:8, suggesting that the second is less characteristically Jewish. Only marginally more convincing are the geographical clues that we have been following already: if the Sea of Galilee has a Jewish side and a Gentile side, and the boat trip in 8:10 takes Jesus back to the Jews (he meets Pharisees in v. 11), we might infer that before v. 10, he was among Gentiles still.

We are persuaded that the feeding of the 4,000 is about Gentile inclusion, but for another reason: its connection to the Syrophoenician woman. We didn't notice this at first, but there's something a bit odd about 7:26–27. To paraphrase: 'Please heal my daughter'; 'Why should I give you any food?' It's a non sequitur. It doesn't seem to fit. How did a request for healing turn into a conversation about who's welcome at the dinner table? It's possible, of course, that this is just poetic licence on Jesus' part. But accomplished users of the **Context tool** or **Structure tool** can't help but wonder: is it significant that a conversation about bread and crumbs comes sandwiched (so to speak!) between two miraculous feedings?

If you're in the habit of using the **Translations tool**, and you read the passage in a more literal translation such as the New American Standard Bible (NASB), then you would find another connection that pushes us to the same conclusion:

5,000	They all ate and were satisfied (6:42)
Woman	'Let the children be satisfied first' (7:27)
4,000	And they ate and were satisfied (8:8)

Mark's intention is clear: he wants us to understand the feeding of the 4,000 in the context of blessing to a Syrophoenician. She asked for crumbs, but she (or at least the Gentiles she represents) got a banquet. And here's the final step in the argument: if the 5,000 is about God's great exodus rescue, then the 4,000 tells us that Gentiles can be rescued too. Dogs can be saved!

This is a point often lost on modern readers, because we (wrongly) presume that Gentiles always had an equal share in God's salvation. In the Old Testament, this was not the case. We forget that, with only a few exceptions, it was Jews (and not Egyptians) who were saved through the parting of the Red Sea;[4] it was Jews (and not Canaanites) who were given the land of milk and honey; it was in defence of the Jews (and against the Philistines) that David went out against Goliath. God's purposes were not ethnically all-inclusive. As the apostle Paul puts it, Gentiles were once 'alienated from the commonwealth of Israel and strangers to the covenants of promise, having no hope and without God in the world' (Ephesians 2:12). But now, with the exorcism of a little girl, a healing of a deaf man and a banquet in the desert, Jesus signals an epoch shift. Gentiles can be rescued too. Dogs can be saved!

With the benefit of hindsight, we can see that Mark had prepared the ground for this in the first part of chapter 7. During Jesus' explanation that our hearts are the source of defilement, rather than the food we eat, Mark inserts an editorial aside: 'Thus he declared all foods clean' (7:19). Why is this significant? Because the previous requirement that Jews eat only kosher food had ensured that they only mixed with kosher people – that is, fellow Jews. (That's why the apostle Peter was horrified when he received a vision suggesting he should enjoy a hog roast with a Gentile centurion – read Acts 10 if you don't know the story). But now bacon sandwiches are OK, and all who trust in Christ can be kosher, regardless of ethnicity.

Do you see what a huge deal this is for all of us who are Gentiles? If Mark had left this section out of his Gospel, we might as well forget anything that we've been excited by so far:

- Jesus is God's King. But Mark means he is the Messiah, the King of the Jews. It's not obvious why that is good news for you, Gentile reader.
- Jesus is bringing in an amazing kingdom with no place for evil spirits, sickness or sin. Shame that you're excluded from citizenship, Gentile reader.
- Jesus has power to save from death. But, Gentile reader, what's to say he has any intention of saving you?

It sounds shocking, doesn't it? Because we had presumed we were included. We had felt a sense of entitlement. We got upset at Jesus calling a woman a dog, and it hadn't even occurred to us that we might be dogs too.

The mistaken assumption that God is obligated to save us lies behind that common objection to Christianity: 'What about tribe x on a desert island who have never heard?' It is said that the failure to save tribe x makes God unfair, whereas in fact, fairness requires only that God gives them what they deserve, which is the same as what we deserve: punishment for our sins. Amazingly, God does want tribe x to hear his gospel and be saved, hence the urgency of world mission. But they have no *right* to hear (just as we had no right), and he has no *obligation* to save them (or to save us). It is pure grace.

To finish with the **Copycat tool**, it's obvious that Mark intends the Syrophoenician woman to be our example. She gets it right, and earns Jesus' commendation. She humbles herself. She comes empty-handed, but she leaves full of blessing. God's rescue extends even to her and her daughter. Dogs can be saved!

Unblinded (8:11–30)

I (Andrew) am red/green colour blind. Just to clarify – because everyone always asks this – yes, I can still use traffic lights. Being colour blind doesn't mean that I can't see in colour. It just means that the contrast between different shades of reds and browns and greens is reduced, and they all get a bit muddy.

Apart from excluding 'airline pilot' from my list of career options and causing a few ill-advised shirt/tie combos, this hasn't been particularly debilitating. The only time it was nearly a problem was when I failed the medical on the first day of my internship at a pharmaceutical company. The task was to match some pairs of coloured wires, most of which seemed, to me, to be an identical shade of brown. It was made worse when, being slightly flustered, I accidentally dropped a few of them onto the carpet, which was also brown (they instantly vanished). Fortunately, since all I was going to be doing in the lab for two months was to make a white powder, I got to keep the internship.

Colour blindness isn't really that serious, although I look forward to my new-creation eyes. Real blindness is much more difficult. But spiritual blindness, as we shall see in this chapter, is the worst of the lot.

You'll have noticed by now that the **Structure tool** is usually the first out of the box. Thinking about the different parts of a passage and how they fit together is indispensable. This time we've left it to you, and it's one of the most important Dig Deeper exercises in this book. Don't skip it, or nothing else will make sense!

DIG DEEPER: **Structure tool** (with apologies to those who remember doing a very similar exercise in the original *Dig Deeper*).

Read through 8:11–30 a couple of times. Can you identify three major sections?

One of Mark's favourite techniques, as we've seen before, is to sandwich three episodes together to point out a connection between them. Can you identify such a connection in this case? How does the middle section help explain what is happening in the outer sections? (We hope that our decision to call this kind of structure a 'sandwich' won't cause any confusion, given all the talk in the passage about bread: that's just a coincidence!)

The sandwich structure is confirmed by Jesus' choice of language in v. 18. What connection is made here between the disciples and the man at Bethsaida?

Finally (with apologies for being slightly Sunday-schoolish about it), fill in the blanks here to spell out the point that Mark is making:

The man at Bethsaida is suffering from _____, but at the end of the episode, he can _____. The disciples in the boat are suffering from _____, but in

Caesarea Philippi, Peter comes to _____. The person who, by miraculous intervention, makes the difference in the case of the man at Bethsaida is _____. By implication, it is also _____ who makes the difference to Peter!

Pray about this, because what you have just discovered is a massive, massive deal.

We could stop right there. By the judicious use of just one tool, you have identified the author's purpose. The only thing to be gained by digging deeper still is that we see this point more vividly. The details will show us that the before was worse than we thought, and the after is more amazing.

The before was worse than we thought

The disciples' situation before Jesus performs a miracle at Bethsaida is worse than we might have thought. But Mark doesn't begin with the disciples. First, we get a cameo appearance by the Pharisees, up to their usual tricks. They make a pretence of spiritual enquiry, but actually, says Mark, they are out to 'test' Jesus (v. 11). Asking for a sign from heaven is a bit rich, given all that they have seen already (e.g. 2:1–11). Yet, instead of following where these signs lead and submitting to Jesus as King, they just hold up more and more hoops for him to jump through. Jesus won't jump: 'Why does this generation seek a sign? Truly, I say to you, no sign will be given to this generation' (8:12). It's always worth thinking about the details. Why didn't Jesus say, 'No sign will be given to *you Pharisees*'? Instead, he says, 'this generation', which suggests that the problem of hard-heartedness is more widespread.

Up to this point, the disciples have been the goodies, and the Pharisees the baddies. But now Jesus is evidently concerned that this distinction may become blurred: 'Watch out,' he says to the disciples, 'beware of the leaven [i.e. the corrupting influence][1] of the Pharisees and the leaven of Herod' (v. 15). We've known from the beginning of the Gospel that the correct response to God's King is to repent and believe (1:15). But the Pharisees seem unable or unwilling to believe, no matter how many signs are multiplied before them. And Herod, although he loved to hear John's message, would not repent. Jesus is warning the disciples – who have heard the message and seen the signs – not to get themselves stuck in the same position.

But then a seemingly trivial conversation about lunch reveals that, despite Jesus' caution, the leaven has spread to the disciples too:

> And they began discussing with one another the fact that they had no bread. And Jesus, aware of this, said to them, 'Why are you discussing the fact that you have no bread? Do you not yet perceive or understand? Are your hearts hardened? Having eyes do you not see, and having ears do you not hear? And do you not remember? When I broke the five loaves for the five thousand, how many baskets full of broken pieces did you take up?' They said to him, 'Twelve.' 'And the seven for the four thousand, how many baskets full of broken pieces did you take up?' And they said to him, 'Seven.' And he said to them, 'Do you not yet understand?' (vv. 16–21)

You don't have to be a genius with the **Tone and Feel tool** to realize that Jesus is upset. He fires a barrage of questions at them, barely pausing to hear their response. Eight questions in four verses. He is incredulous at their ignorance. 'Do you not yet UNDERSTAND?!'

But to find out why he's upset, we need to get out the **Context tool**. This comes into its own here, because several strands that have been woven through the wider section all come together, as we've tried to illustrate in this little diagram:

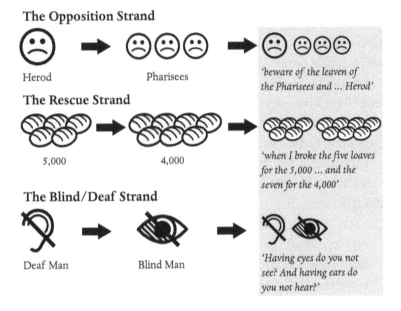

The Opposition Strand

Herod   Pharisees   'beware of the leaven of the Pharisees and ... Herod'

The Rescue Strand

5,000   4,000   'when I broke the five loaves for the 5,000 ... and the seven for the 4,000'

The Blind/Deaf Strand

Deaf Man   Blind Man   'Having eyes do you not see? And having ears do you not hear?'

Having begun to discuss the opposition strand already, let's turn to the rescue strand (although very soon, these different strands will start to interweave). The feeding of the 5,000 has been one of the high points of the story so far, as Jesus identifies himself as the bringer of a new exodus. Then came the feeding of the 4,000, where the doors of this rescue were thrown open to Gentiles too. Wonderful news for all who believe. But this was just the problem. The disciples *didn't* believe.

You could understand the disciples' incredulity in 6:37, when Jesus suggested that they should find a way of feeding the crowd – they didn't yet know that Jesus had planned a miracle. It was more worrying when *after* the miracle, Mark tells us that 'they did not understand about the loaves' (6:52). It was more worrying still when, at the feeding of the 4,000, they were again confused about how a crowd might be fed (8:4). Erm, he-llo? We're in a desolate place, with some loaves and fish and a guy who specializes in miracles? Is this not sounding a little familiar? But they draw a blank. It's most worrying of all when we find the disciples in a boat feeling peckish, with a single loaf of bread. This is by far the best hungry-mouths-to-available-food ratio that Jesus has faced. It's obvious that 'the feeding of the twelve' will be a doddle. But, incredibly, the disciples still don't get it.

Perhaps the disciples are not the sharpest knives in the drawer. Perhaps they are a few loaves short of a picnic (OK, OK, enough bread puns for now). And yet they can recall even the most specific details about the earlier feedings. 'How many baskets of leftovers did you collect?' And without hesitation they answer, 'Twelve.' 'Seven.' There seems to be no problem here with their memory or their intellect. So, why don't they get it?

Everything in the passage points to the uncomfortable truth that their ignorance stems from rebellion and sin. They are not innocently, naively ignorant. They are culpably, wilfully ignorant. Only this makes sense of Jesus' earlier warning: 'Beware.' Only this makes sense of his anger – he would never raise his voice at people simply because they were dim. Only this makes sense of his vocabulary: 'Are your hearts hardened?' (8:17; see also 6:52). Hard-heartedness was characteristic of Pharaoh in the Old Testament, and is characteristic of the Pharisees and Herodians here in Mark (3:1–6). Hard-heartedness stands for seeing more and more signs, but refusing to repent and believe.

We turn finally to the blind/deaf strand. As you will have noted in the last Dig Deeper exercise, Jesus uses the physical predicament of the deaf and blind men as a metaphor for the spiritual condition of the disciples: 'Having eyes do you not see, and having ears do you not hear?' This really is a bad situation. It's not just that they are a bit slow and need more time to figure stuff out. It's not just that their spiritual education is incomplete and they need more information. They are *blind*. They have no more chance of grasping it than I (Andrew) had of matching coloured wires. It is impossible.

Again, ignorance is tinged with culpability. It turns out (thanks, cross-reference column in our Bible!) that Jesus is using a phrase already coined by the prophets Jeremiah and Ezekiel, and when we went digging with the **Quotation/Allusion tool**, we found that it was *guilty* people who were described as blind and deaf:

> 'As you have forsaken me and served foreign gods in your land,
> so you shall serve foreigners in a land that is not yours.'
>> Declare this in the house of Jacob;
>>> proclaim it in Judah:
>> 'Hear this, O foolish and senseless people,
>>> who have eyes, but see not,
>>> who have ears, but hear not.'
> (Jeremiah 5:19–21)

> The word of the LORD came to me: 'Son of man, you dwell
> in the midst of a rebellious house, who have eyes to see, but
> see not, who have ears to hear, but hear not, for they are a
> rebellious house.'
> (Ezekiel 12:1–2)

The point is amply made already. But we could go on. When explaining his rationale for speaking in parables back in Mark 4:10–12, Jesus had quoted from Isaiah chapter 6 – 'they may indeed see and not perceive, and may indeed hear but not understand'. It was God's judgment on morally culpable people to blind and deafen them. And blindness even turns up in Isaiah 29:9–14, which Jesus had quoted against the Pharisees in Mark 7:6–7 – the passage that emphasized their culpability more than any other.

Thus the various strands weave together into a grim tapestry. The disciples have been offered an exodus rescue, if only they would repent and believe. But the Herod-like unrepentance and Pharisee-like unbelief have infected them. The disciples are hard-hearted. They are blind and deaf. More signs won't help at this stage – they don't see them. Further explanations are ineffective – they go unheard. The disciples are in terrible trouble. And so were we.

The before was worse than we thought.

The after is more amazing than we thought

Just as the predicament of the deaf man and the blind man formed one of the strands that wove together to describe the disciples' problem, so Jesus' healings of these men herald the solution. In 8:22–26, we meet someone with a real medical condition (perhaps corneal opacity or damaged retinal ganglion cells), who can suddenly see people and colours and beauty. What does Jesus do to achieve this change? He spits. This is a miracle. There is, of course, the puzzling detail that the man doesn't see clearly straight away; he experiences an intermediate stage where he can make out 'men, but they look like trees, walking' (v. 24). For now, we'll simply mark this in the margin as 'AFL' (awaiting further light). But intermediate stage or not, unblinding (or undeafening)[2] someone is pretty amazing.

It's amazing physically, but it points to an even more amazing spiritual reality: Jesus miraculously opens Peter's eyes to see who Jesus is. Before the miracle, Peter is clueless. Asking him, 'Who do you say I am?' would be like asking your chihuahua to help you with *The Times* crossword. But after the miracle, he has his eureka moment: 'You are the Christ.'

Finally! YES! As readers, we've known that Jesus is the 'Christ, the Son of God' since Mark's opening line, but this is the first time that anyone in the narrative itself, bar evil spirits, has got it. (Flick back to 'Getting started' if you need to refresh your memory about the three confessions that form the backbone of the Gospel as a whole.) We have reached a major turning point.

Of course, Mark teases us a bit. Before we hear those wonderful words, 'the Christ', on Peter's lips, we have to sit through a survey of some of the wrong answers doing the rounds – 'John the Baptist', 'Elijah', 'one of the prophets'. If your **Context tool** antennae are properly attuned, then you will realize that we've heard these exact answers before in 6:14–16 in connection with Mr Unrepentance himself. The effect is to make the reader uneasy. Are the disciples doomed to the same confusion? And perhaps even for the same reasons? Is the yeast of Herod still at work? And then, just as we are feeling at our most pessimistic, Peter gets it.

Why does Peter get it? Not because he is more insightful than the others, or less unrepentant. Not even because witnessing one more miracle finally made the difference. It's because a miracle happened to him. Jesus granted him spiritual sight.

Remember that Peter's blindness was culpable. Remember that it was bound up with hard-heartedness. Remember that it threatened to cut him off from the rescue that the loaves and fishes had signified. Opened eyes speak of mercy as well as revelation. They speak of a softened heart as well as an enlightened mind. In fact, Isaiah, whose exposition of the problem of blindness we have already considered, would say that opened eyes mean the arrival of God's long-promised salvation:

> 'Be strong; fear not!
> Behold, your God
>   will come with vengeance,
> with the recompense of God.
>   He will come and save you.'
> Then the eyes of the blind shall be opened,
>   and the ears of the deaf unstopped;
> then shall the lame man leap like a deer,
>   and the tongue of the mute sing for joy.
> (Isaiah 35:4–6)

It's time for the **'So What?' tool**, as we begin to apply these lessons to ourselves. Who do *you* say that Jesus is? If you answer, 'the Christ', it is only because he has miraculously opened your eyes. It's not because:

- You were more intelligent than the next person: 'I got a first in theology from Oxford, and so I worked out who Jesus is.'
- You were less Herod-like than the next person: 'Repentance wasn't an issue for me, because I naturally chose to live the right way.'
- You were less Pharisee-like than the next person: 'I always follow evidence objectively, and so I readily embraced Jesus as my King.'

Whenever you hear someone giving their testimony as if they are the hero of the story, or as if the decisive factor in becoming a Christian had something to do with them, then they haven't learned the lesson of the blind man. A truly Christian testimony goes more like this:

> Amazing grace! How sweet the sound
> That saved a wretch like me!
> I once was lost, but now am found;
> Was blind, but now I see.[3]

Or like this:

> I sought the Lord, and afterward I knew
> He moved my soul to seek Him, seeking me.
> It was not I that found, O Saviour true;
> No, I was found of Thee.[4]

Come die with me (8:31 – 9:29)

The Son of Man must die before he rises

As we write this, we're halfway through our Friday morning book-writing session, and as a bit of a special treat, we're pausing to sample a rather fine selection of cheeses – Montgomery Cheddar, Comté, Gouda and three soft cheeses, one of which is so pongy that it opened the fridge door by itself. We don't dine in luxury like this every week, but having just heard Peter confess Jesus as 'the Christ', we thought it a suitable moment for celebration!

What Jesus says next would be like finding a live scorpion on the cheeseboard. It's hard to imagine a bigger shock:

> And he began to teach them that the Son of Man must suffer many things and be rejected by the elders and the chief priests and the scribes and be killed, and after three days rise again.
> (8:31)

To feel more deeply the scandal of what Jesus is saying, we need to understand what is meant by the title, 'Son of Man'. Time for you to dig deeper with the **Vocabulary tool**.

DIG DEEPER: **Vocabulary tool**

Option 1 (the lazy shortcut): Look up 'Son of Man' in a Bible dictionary. What ideas are associated with this title? How does a fuller appreciation of the title make Jesus' words in 8:31 even more shocking?

Option 2 (doing for yourself what the writers of the Bible dictionary did): Use the **Context tool** to explore how the title has been used previously in Mark. What ideas are associated with 'Son of Man' in 2:10 and 2:28? Use the **Quotation/ Allusion tool** to consider the background of the title in Daniel 7:13–14.[1] How does a fuller appreciation of the title make Jesus' words in 8:31 even more shocking?

If the news of Jesus' impending death doesn't shock us as much as it should, that's because we already know how the story ends (and because Mark has already dropped several hints to prepare us for it – see e.g. 2:20, 3:19, 6:14–29). But put yourself in Peter's shoes for a moment. His head is full of the idea of 'Christ' – king, ruler, rescuer. When he tries to put this alongside 'suffer, rejected, killed', it just doesn't fit. It's like trying to combine 'celebration' and 'cancer', or 'beautiful' and 'bomb aftermath'. 'Christ' and 'die' don't go together. It would have seemed crazy to Peter that *Jesus* – the one who walked away unscathed from an encounter with a legion of demons – could be endangered by a bunch of chief priests. It would have seemed absurd that *Jesus* – who had raised Jairus' daughter from the dead – could himself die.

Notice that Jesus doesn't say merely that the Son of Man 'will die' – as if he had become aware of the plot against him (3:6) and was feeling pessimistic about the outcome. No, he goes further than this. He says that he 'must' die. Mark won't tell us why for another two chapters. But he does let us feel the full force of Jesus' rebuke to Peter; any suggestion that the crucifixion could be avoided comes from the devil himself.

This is a good time for an aside on what is sometimes called the 'Messianic Secret'. You'll probably have noticed, while reading through Mark, that Jesus has issued gagging orders on demons who try to declare his identity (1:34; 3:12), that he instructs witnesses of miracles to keep schtum about what they saw or avoid people (1:44; 5:43; 7:36; 8:26), and that when Peter finally confesses him as the Christ, he 'strictly charged them to tell no one about him' (8:30). This secrecy is puzzling – how come Jesus doesn't want to be famous? Bottles of theological ink have been spilt over this issue. The most straightforward explanation is that he doesn't want to go public with only half the story. If the news gets out that he is 'Christ', then the Jewish nationalists will make him the champion of their own agenda; miraculous powers would come in handy in overthrowing the Roman occupation! But the full story is not about a political Christ, but about a Christ who must suffer. Only when the disciples have grasped this (as Peter, for one, certainly hasn't) will they be ready to preach the news far and wide.

Jesus has shocked everyone by linking 'Son of Man' with suffering. But the story won't end there. He will rise from the dead (8:31). He will return 'in the glory of his Father with the holy angels' (8:38). As the prophet Daniel saw, Jesus will still be given:

> dominion
> and glory and a kingdom,
> that all peoples, nations, and languages
> should serve him;

his dominion is an everlasting dominion,
    which shall not pass away,[2]
and his kingdom one
    that shall not be destroyed.
(Daniel 7:14)

Christians must die before they rise

Ernest Shackleton, the famous Antarctic explorer, reportedly placed the following text in a newspaper: 'Men wanted for hazardous journey. Small wages. Bitter cold. Long months of complete darkness. Constant danger. Safe return doubtful. Honour and recognition in case of success.'

It might not have been the kind of advert to get people applying in droves, but there is a place for honesty. Shackleton's expedition turned out to be an utter nightmare. His ship, appropriately named *Endurance*, was frozen solid in a sheet of ice for nearly nine months. Just as things were looking up, and the ice began to melt, the ship sprang a leak and began to sink. After several more months camping out on ice floes, the crew had no choice but to send a rescue party in a tiny lifeboat in hurricane-force winds to a whaling station 800 nautical miles away. Shackleton had warned that it would be grim. He was right.

Jesus' invitation to would-be disciples is similarly frank: 'If anyone would come after me, let him deny himself and take up his cross and follow me' (8:34). We easily miss the force of this, because 'take up your cross' has entered the English language as an idiom for anything moderately unpleasant that has to be done – putting out the bins, kissing the great aunt with the moustache, filing your tax return. The original sense may be better captured thus: 'If anyone would come after me, let him deny himself and strap himself into his electric chair and follow me.' Jesus is inviting us to put ourselves on death row.

The **Context tool** reminds us that Jesus is not asking us to do anything he is not willing to do himself, because vv. 34–38 (about discipleship) immediately follow vv. 31–33 (about Jesus' own death). Indeed, the two paragraphs are bracketed together (**Structure tool**) by 'Son of Man' bookends to keep them connected in our minds. Notice also (**Vocabulary tool**) the decision to use the word 'cross' when describing the disciples' possible fate, even though we know that in reality, some were martyred by other means (for example, Stephen was stoned, and James was put to the sword; see Acts 7:58–60; 12:2). In various ways, then, Mark has set out to underline the parallel between Jesus' fate and the fate of those who would 'come after' him.

We might say, in summary, that the Christian life is 'cross-shaped'. For many throughout history, and in some parts of the world today, following Jesus has meant actual martyrdom. It is, at the very least, a call to radical self-denial. Be prepared to deny yourself in your career, your popularity, your use of money, your sex life, your aspirations to an easy life. We shall see Jesus touching on many of these areas as we read on.

If the Christian life is that difficult, why would anyone sign up? The 'for' of v. 35 will have experienced toolkit users already reaching for the **Linking Words tool**, as it introduces a two-edged motivation. If you try to save your life now (i.e. you avoid the cost of following Jesus), then you'll lose it in the future; if you lose your life for Jesus' sake and the gospel's, then you will save it. We have tried to illustrate this reversal of fortunes in a diagram. Pause and meditate on this for a few minutes, because this is a truth that should change lives.

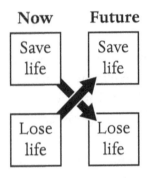

Next we get three more 'for's in vv. 36–38, which expand (somewhat scarily) on the top-left-to-bottom-right axis of the diagram. What would be the point of saving your life – even gaining the whole world – and then losing your very soul? You get the best degree from the best university, and so you get a place with the best law firm. You wear the best suits and drive the best car, and you live in the best flat with the best postcode. You win the best girl or the best guy, and enjoy the best marriage with the best children, who get into the best schools and get the best grades. Having invested in the best pension, you enjoy the best retirement and play the best golf. You have the best funeral with the best coffin. What would be the point? And when it comes to judgment, what exactly are you hoping to bargain with to get your soul back? Although you escape the shame that comes with aligning yourself with the Bible's teaching ('me and . . . my words', v. 38), you will be shamed by Jesus when he comes in glory.

When we teach this at our church, we get people to fold or cover the page so that the right-hand side of the diagram is hidden, and you can see only the 'now' column. You are faced with a simple choice: would you rather save your life or lose your life? It's a no-brainer. Of course you save your life. If this world is all there is, self-sacrifice is for idiots. But now unfold or uncover the page and ask yourself the same question. Again, it's a no-brainer, but the opposite way round. Of course you lose your life. No sacrifice is too great if eternal glory is on offer, while no temporary pleasure could be worth eternal loss. The paper-folding illustration shows us this: the choice of a rational person depends entirely on whether he or she believes in the right-hand side of the diagram. It depends entirely on whether he or she thinks that the Son of Man rose again.

The resurrection of Jesus actually underpins both of the future boxes. It assures those who follow Jesus to the grave that they too can expect life beyond it (top right box), because he has set the precedent. But it also establishes Jesus as the Son of Man who will come in judgment (bottom right box).

Whiter than white

The action quickly moves on, and we find Jesus up a mountain. Some pretty crazy stuff happens. Two dead guys appear,[3] Jesus is transfigured before the disciples' eyes, and God's voice booms down from the clouds. We could draw all sorts of random lessons from this episode,[4] but, as always, we need to be disciplined and let the **Author's Purpose tool** guide us. Why is Mark including this episode with these details *here*, and what point is he making? We came up with two possibilities that we're going to call the 'listen-to-Jesus' theory and the 'future-glory-is-real' theory.

Let's take the 'listen-to-Jesus' theory first. This gives most weight to the words spoken from heaven in 9:7, which seems fair enough given that . . . well, given that they are words spoken from heaven! God the Father repeats his affirmation of Jesus as his 'beloved Son' (see 1:11), and tells us to pay attention to what Jesus says. So far, so good. But some people want to go further, and infer from the sudden disappearance of Moses and Elijah (taken to represent the Law and the

Prophets, respectively) that God is saying, 'Listen to Jesus, because he replaces the Old Testament.' That doesn't stand up to scrutiny. First, you'd expect v. 7 and v. 8 to be the other way round. Secondly, the very next thing that Jesus says is about the importance of the Old Testament (see vv. 11–13). It's much better to use the **Context tool** and consider the command to 'listen' in the light of what Jesus has just said in 8:31–38. God the Father is underlining the pattern of suffering before glory, both for his own Son and for the disciples. Perhaps we should call it the 'listen-to-what-Jesus-says-about-dying-and-rising' theory.

It's always tempting to go with your first credible answer, but sometimes there is something even better out there if you keep digging. Verse 9 got us thinking – if this is all about listening, why the emphasis on what they had 'seen' (see also vv. 4, 8)? Hmm. Well, what did they see exactly? A change in Jesus' appearance that Mark describes like a slogan for a washing powder: 'Persil. For clothes intensely white, as no-one on earth could bleach them.' In a laundry commercial, this would be hyperbole, but what if Mark intends us to read it literally? What if he says 'no-one on earth' because they have seen a glimpse of heaven? That would explain the brief appearance of Moses and Elijah, who presumably are in heaven now. It would also explain the way in which Jesus connects the transfiguration with the resurrection in v. 9. What the disciples have glimpsed, it seems, is a sneak preview of Jesus' resurrection life, of the glory that is to come. That's how we arrived at our 'future-glory-is-real' theory.

This theory also makes good sense of Jesus' enigmatic statement that 'there are some standing here who will not taste death until they *see* the kingdom of God after it has come with power' (9:1, italics added). There have been various suggestions as to what powerful coming is in view, but isn't it most obviously a reference to the foretaste of glory that three of the disciples are about to receive on the mountain? The very specific link of 'after six days' (v. 2) and the fact that only some of the hearers of v. 1 are with him to 'see' it suggests that this is the case.

As a cherry on the top, have a look at 2 Peter 1:16–18. (We are wary of random cross-references, but having enjoyed a Mark cake with Mark icing, we thought we might just allow a 2 Peter cherry). Years later, when Peter wants to reassure his readers that Jesus will come again in glory, it is the trans-figuration he points to. Being there on that day had convinced him that future glory is real.

Let's again use the **Context tool** to consider how 'future-glory-is-real' might fit with Mark 8:31–38. It's actually pretty obvious. The motivation for the disciples to take up their cross and follow Jesus was all to do with glory in the future. But what if the 'future' doesn't happen? What if it's just pie in the sky? Worry not. On the mountain, the disciples have already seen the future. So, you can be sure that taking up your cross will be worth it.

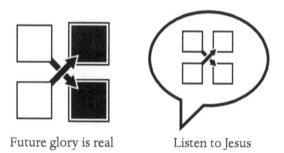

Future glory is real   Listen to Jesus

So then, votes please. Hands up for the 'listen-to-Jesus' theory? Hands up for the 'future-glory-is-real' theory?

On this occasion, it doesn't seem necessary to choose. The two theories dovetail nicely, because, in their own way, each underlines the message of 8:35.

As it is written of him

Andrew owns a little jar of Montezuma coffee pips, each one of which is a double espresso condensed into a boiled sweet. If you have something similar in your cupboard, please eat several of them now. We are coming up to one of the trickiest paragraphs in Mark.

As they head down the mountain, the disciples are trying to make sense of what they've just seen, but they get stuck. Isn't Elijah supposed to come before the kingdom of God arrives? (They get this from the 'scribes', who presumably got it from Malachi 4:5). As readers, we are ahead of the disciples, because we know that John the Baptist has already come as the new Elijah (remember the camel's-hair tunic and leather belt outfit in Mark 1:6?). But Jesus steers the conversation in a different direction:

> And how is it written of the Son of Man that he should suffer many things and be treated with contempt? But I tell you that Elijah has come, and they did to him whatever they pleased, as it is written of him.
>
> (9:12–13)

Jesus' focus is on the inevitability of his suffering. It must happen because 'it is written'. Later in his Gospel, Mark will point us to passages like Psalm 22 and Zechariah 13:7, which clearly speak of a suffering Messiah. But here Jesus makes the point by drawing a parallel between himself and Elijah: 'it is written of the Son of Man . . . it is written of him [Elijah].'

Where do we see Elijah's suffering written of and then fulfilled? Jesus is drawing a second parallel: John the Baptist suffered at the hands of Herodias, the evil wife of King Herod, just as it was written that Elijah had suffered at the hands of

Jezebel, the evil wife of King Ahab. Perhaps you remember this from when we were digging in Mark chapter 6?

And then perhaps you also remember the various ways in which John's execution anticipated the crucifixion of Jesus. Both involved opportunistic plots, corrupt judges capitulating to peer pressure, and faithful disciples laying bodies in tombs.

Still with us? Basically Elijah, John and Jesus are all inter-related in a triangle of comparisons. Jesus will suffer as was written of Elijah. John suffered like Elijah. Jesus will suffer like John. The bottom line? Suffering is inevitable. It was written. It must be fulfilled.

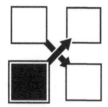

Suffering is necessary

To wrap up, let's again use the **Context tool** to think about how this relates to 8:31–38. Certainly it underlines the 'must suffer many things' of Jesus' fate (8:31). But in doing so, it spills over to any disciple who would 'take up his cross and follow [Jesus]' (8:34). Those who follow a suffering Messiah, heralded by a suffering Baptist, foreshadowed by a suffering prophet, can expect to suffer. This might seem gloomy, but Mark knows, like Shackleton, that realistic expectations are crucial to survival when life gets tough. Be reassured: the road to glory was always supposed to begin this way.

'I believe; help my unbelief!'

We come finally to a heart-wrenching description of a

young boy in the grip of an evil spirit bent on destroying him. This is one of those cases where a dispassionate summary won't do – 'Disciples fail in exorcisms of boy, but Jesus succeeds.' The longer-than-usual descriptions are our cue to get out the **Tone and Feel tool**, as Mark pushes us to engage at an emotional level. It begins with a report from the boy's father:

> [H]e has a spirit that makes him mute. And whenever it seizes him, it throws him down, and he foams and grinds his teeth and becomes rigid.
>
> (9:17–18)

But then, having heard about these manifestations, we see them happening live: 'when the spirit saw [Jesus], immediately it convulsed the boy, and he fell on the ground and rolled about, foaming at the mouth' (v. 20). Finally, in v. 22, the full horror of the situation becomes clear. The spirit had 'often cast him into fire and into water, to destroy him'. All toddlers need to be warned away from fireplaces, but can you even imagine one who, possessed of a destructive spirit, does his best to hurl himself into them? Or can you conceive of family holidays by the seaside, in which you constantly have to restrain your son from drowning himself? The situation is desperate. But Jesus is powerful to save.

One thing we couldn't help noticing about the exorcism itself was Mark's unusual choice of vocabulary: the boy resembled a 'corpse', and people said, 'He is dead', but Jesus 'lifted him up, and he arose' (vv. 26–27). Why does Mark describe an exorcism as if it were a resurrection? We already know that Jesus has power over death (and indeed the boy's restoration sounds very like the raising of Jairus' daughter in

5:41), but Mark seeks an opportunity to underline that truth again. Why? The **Context tool** provides a ready answer: having invited his followers to lose their lives for his sake and the gospel's, Jesus reassures us that he has power to raise us again.

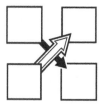

Jesus can raise you

But some details of the text remain unaccounted for, which is a sign that there is more digging to be done. The **Repetition tool** alerted us to an emphasis on faith/belief – 'O faithless generation' (9:19); 'All things are possible for one who believes' (v. 23); 'I believe; help my unbelief!' (v. 24); and perhaps even 'This kind cannot be driven out by anything but prayer', if prayer is the proper expression of faith (v. 29). The point seems clear – the right course of action is to trust Jesus, even when that is hard. The disciples apparently fail to trust him, neither praying nor seeking his help when their own efforts are unsuccessful. But the boy's father is a candidate for the **Copycat tool**. He does trust Jesus, albeit waveringly. And as he acknowledges his weakness and pleads with Jesus for help in believing, he shows us the model response.

Let's draw all the threads of this breathtakingly important chapter together. The Son of Man must suffer before he enters his glory. Any who would come after him must deny themselves, take up their cross and follow him. For whoever wants to save their life will lose it. But whoever loses their life for Jesus' sake and the gospel will save it. We must listen to Jesus. We should take encouragement from the disciples'

mountaintop glimpse of heavenly glory. We should understand from the Scriptures that suffering was always the plan.
We should reflect on Jesus' ability to raise the dead. And we
should pray: 'Lord Jesus, you have promised that those who
lose their life for you and the gospel will save it. I believe.
Help my unbelief.'

The eye of a needle (9:30 – 10:31)

Tim was reading the Reformation21 blog (which we recommend, incidentally), and came across this:

> There are a few things that frustrate me about a number of the books that I have read recently . . . [One is] where the author clearly subscribes to the 'open with an illustration' school of preaching and feels obliged to start with some allegedly gripping anecdote which is then mercilessly wrestled into position and bound, sometimes by very tenuous threads, to the point of the chapter. After twenty such excursions on the trot, one becomes weary.[1]

Oh dear. Sorry! Better get straight into the chapter.

As always, we need the **Structure tool** to get our bearings. We've often thought about the structure of a particular section, but actually we can apply the tool at lots of different levels: the whole Gospel, the chapter, the paragraph and even the sentence. It's a bit like Google Earth. You zoom in and zoom out, and see different amounts of detail, depending on your level of magnification.

Let's begin with the whole of Mark. This is like viewing the whole of the UK on your screen. You can't make out individual towns and villages, but you can see overall features like the foot of Cornwall or the bump of Norfolk. At this level of zoom, we can see that we are in a section bracketed by two healings of blind men, in which Jesus three times predicts his own death and resurrection, each time following the prediction with instructions for Christian living (chapters 8 – 10).

Now let's zoom in on the south-east of England, so that we can see the M25 and the loop in the Thames that you probably recognize from *EastEnders*. We're now focused on the second of Jesus' predictions of his death (9:30–32) and the accompanying teaching on discipleship (9:33 – 10:31). We are reminded of the close connection between Jesus' own sacrifice and the sacrifices he asks of his followers (just as in 8:31–38). At this level of zoom, we also notice that the teaching on discipleship is bracketed by two references to the 'last' being 'first' (see 9:35 and 10:31). This reversal of fortunes is reminiscent of Jesus' earlier promise that 'whoever loses his life . . . will save it' (8:35, **Context tool**). Looking between the bookends, the idea of being 'last' seems to be fleshed out in terms of serving others ahead of ourselves.

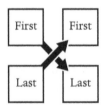

Next, we zoom in on east London and see the Mile End Road and Stepney Green Tube station. Subdividing at this level becomes tricky: we get teaching on receiving children, responding to Christian competition, fighting sin, salt, divorce, children again, a rich man who has kept (some of) the commandments, an impossibility regarding a camel, a promise to Peter. All this content has something to do with denying oneself, but there isn't anything that jumps out at us as an obvious structural marker, other than maybe the change of location in 10:1. Let's break it there, but only tentatively, lest, in our overeagerness to systematize, we devise a structure more precise than even Mark had in mind!

Serving and severing

Picture the scene. As they pass through Galilee, Jesus is teaching the disciples again about his impending death. But there's whispering in the back row. When Jesus asks, as has many a schoolteacher, whether they would care to share the joke with everyone else, they are tongue-tied (9:34). The shameful truth is that even as Jesus had been speaking about self-sacrifice, they had been squabbling about which of them was the greatest. By way of rebuke, Jesus announces the bookend principle: 'If anyone would be first, he must be last of all and servant of all' (v. 35). To illustrate this, Jesus says that they should be willing to receive children, regarded as the least in society. We might paraphrase: 'If you want to be greatest, start changing some nappies.'

When the disciples finally pipe up, it is to tell Jesus about an exorcist whose ministry they've tried to shut down because he didn't belong to their inner circle ('he was not following *us*', 9:38; contrast 8:34). The **Repetition tool** helps us to see their error, because the criterion for fellowship ought to be simply whether someone is acting *in Jesus' name* (9:37, 38 and 39). Just as Jesus had highlighted the need to welcome children, so here he teaches the need to welcome fellow Christians. The exorcist had been doing genuine kingdom work and should not have been stopped.

Time for a quick use of the **'So What?' tool** as we reflect on how readily we find fault with the church down the road, whose ministry is thriving, while ours limps along. Jesus isn't suggesting, of course, that we abandon all discernment – he was happy to call a spade a spade when it came to false teaching (e.g. 7:1–13). But we must search our hearts lest some of our theological quibbles are a mask for our pride, a way of preserving us and ours as the only true believers.

The paragraph ends on a positive note (9:41). Even the smallest act of service towards a fellow Christian will be rewarded.[2] It's a reminder of the right-hand side of our little diagram. There is a future day on which every act of sacrifice will turn to glory. The last will be first.

The next paragraph is one of the most shocking and gruesome in the whole of Jesus' teaching. The film version would carry an 18 certificate and the advice: 'contains strong language and violence of a graphic nature'. Jesus speaks of gouging out eyes and severing limbs. He refers to the 'unquenchable fire' (v. 44) that burns in hell. Using imagery borrowed from the prophet Isaiah, he speaks of bodies festering with worms for ever (Isaiah 66:24). Sometimes people rush to reassure us that this is only 'figurative' (**Genre tool**), and in some ways they are right – Jesus is not expecting Christians to perform literal amputations. But it's a mistake to equate 'figurative' with 'unreal'. It's possible to use metaphor to speak about reality. And if Jesus chooses scary metaphors, it's surely because he wants to warn us of a scary reality.

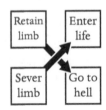

The warning comes in the form of a series of 'it-is-better' comparisons (**Repetition tool**, vv. 42–47) that contrast choices now with outcomes in the future. We've seen the pattern before with save life/lose life, and first/last. This time, we are told that we can keep our bodies intact and 'be thrown into hell', or cut bits off and 'enter life'.[3] By cutting off your hand, or plucking out your eye, Jesus presumably means *taking the most radical action possible* to avoid sin. Taking action that costs you. Perhaps even hurts you. Are you willing to do that? As before, we invite you to fold or cover the page to conceal the right-hand side of the little diagram above. With only 'now' in view, you would be mad to sever your limbs. Why fight sin, if this world is all there is? But then factor in the future, and it's obvious that radical self-denial is 'better'. Entering the kingdom of God bruised and battle-weary is better than hell.

This hill, though high, I covet to ascend;
The difficulty will not me offend.
For I perceive the way to life lies here.
Come, pluck up, heart; let's neither faint
    nor fear.
Better, though difficult, the right way to go,
Than wrong, though easy, where the end
    is woe.[4]

In case you wondered why we plunged straight into vv. 43–48 without discussing v. 42 (and you are right to hold us to account on such things), then it's because we had once again used the **Structure tool**. In Google Earth terms, we're now zoomed in so far that we can see the fishpond and the dilapidated shed covered with blackberries in Andrew's back garden. But even at the level of a paragraph, structure can be really useful. It seems to go like this:

Don't cause other Christians to sin (v. 42)
Be radical with your own sin (vv. 43–49)
Be at peace with other Christians (v. 50)[5]

The juxtaposition tells us that fighting our own sin is bound up with our service of others. If people at church see my reluctance to chop off a hand, then they will be reluctant to chop off a hand. Both of us will compromise together, and I bear some responsibility for their fall. Not only does sin put us in danger as individuals, but also it endangers other Christians. Putting sin to death and living a godly, 'salty' life is the key to a peaceful, united church.

DIG DEEPER: **'So What?'** tool

Think of an area of temptation.
What would be the 'cutting-off-the-hand' equivalent?
How could you deal with it radically? (E.g. if the issue were pornography, you could sell your computer.)
How could your failure to deal with this issue cause other 'little ones' to sin?

We wonder whether all of this has made you feel uncomfortable. Perhaps not, because you have taken Jesus to mean: 'Fighting sin is an optional extra for Christian discipleship, and it would be a bonus if we made some progress in a couple of areas.' But that isn't what he says. He says that unless we stop sinning, we shall find ourselves in hell. Of course, we know the wonderful end of the story – that Jesus dies on the cross to save us from hell. But we mustn't jump the gun. Mark hasn't yet given us the reassurance that everything will be OK. For now, he wants us to feel the sharp edges of Jesus' words: failure to deny yourself is desperately serious.

You who boast in the law dishonour God by breaking the law

A change of location announces the new subsection (10:1), and we are plunged immediately into a controversy about divorce. Cue the sinister music when we realize the question is posed by the Pharisees, who seek 'to test him' (v. 2; see 8:11). Here they are again, up to their usual tricks. But Jesus turns the tables and quizzes them on their understanding of the Law of Moses. They seem pretty sure of themselves as they trot out a quotation from Deuteronomy 24:1–4, but, oh dear, they didn't use the **Context tool**! They picked out a verse that mentions divorce certificates, and conclude that God is happy about divorce certificates. No, says Jesus. 'Because of your hardness of heart he wrote you this commandment' (10:5). In other words, such laws were only necessary because you do things that God *isn't* happy about. If you'd read Deuteronomy in the context of Genesis 2:24, you would know that in creation, God designed marriage to be a lifelong union, that man must not divide what God has joined together, that divorce is deeply wrong.

When we read that 'in the house the disciples asked him again about this matter' (Mark 10:10), we are reminded that, ever since 4:10–12, Jesus' loyal followers have been privy to explanations from which outsiders are excluded. In 7:17–23, this meant that they got more sin-diagnosis than anyone else. Similarly, here, it's the disciples who are shown the full horror of divorce. It leads to adultery, says Jesus.[6] It's a Ten Commandments issue.

This is serious. The Pharisees began the chapter thinking, 'The law is on our side', because they had set the bar so low.

But, as Jesus raises the bar, it's not just the Pharisees who are in trouble: even among his professed followers, there are many who don't clear it. Perhaps you are reading this book as a divorcee, and Jesus' words are not easy for you. Many others (including both authors) will be conscious of past failures in the area of relationships. If only Jesus had caveated his words by saying, 'Here is a Christian ideal, and don't worry too much if you fall short.' But that isn't what he says. In time, Mark will disclose a wonderful remedy for wounded consciences. But as we have already said, we mustn't jump the gun. For now, he wants us to feel the sharp edges of Jesus' words; failure to deny yourself is desperately serious.

Some children now arrive on the scene. Jesus has recently taught the importance of receiving children, and even went so far as to say that receiving children = receiving Jesus = receiving God (**Context tool**, 9:36–37). But what do the disciples do? They 'rebuked them' (10:13). Jesus is indignant. The disciples *shouldn't* have hindered the exorcist, and they *shouldn't* hinder the children, and they *should* be putting themselves last. Jesus ups the stakes with a stern warning: 'Truly, I say to you, whoever does not receive the kingdom of God like a child shall not enter it' (v. 15). This makes us uncomfortable. We want Jesus to say, 'Giving up your status, putting yourself last, coming like a child is the ideal for particularly keen Christians to aspire to.' But he doesn't say that. He says 'unless' and 'shall not enter'. Get this wrong, and forfeit your place in God's kingdom, he says. And the disciples seem to be getting things dangerously wrong.

So, along comes Mr Nice Guy (10:17–22), and we wonder for a moment whether we have met the one who will clear the bar. He's got everything going for him. He treats Jesus with great respect (v. 17). He has kept God's law diligently all his adult life. Hearing this, Jesus 'loved him' (v. 21). But by the end of the paragraph, Mr Nice Guy chooses to walk away from the offer of eternal life that he had sought in the first place.

What is it that Mr Nice Guy gets wrong?

Many people instinctively label his problem as legalism. They smell a theological rat as soon as he asks, 'What must I *do* to inherit eternal life?' Aha! He shouldn't have been trying to *do* anything! Salvation is by faith apart from works (cf. Romans 3:27–28; Galatians 2:16; Titus 3:5).

The problem with this interpretation is . . . it doesn't arise from the text. It is an example of reading in our existing doctrinal framework rather than reading out what Mark has to say. Don't mishear us: we are fully committed to the doctrine of justification by faith alone, and we can be sure that nothing Mark teaches will ultimately contradict Romans or Galatians or Titus. But if we impose our framework too quickly, before we have let Mark speak for himself, then we are in danger of missing anything new that he might want to say, or a different way in which he might want to say it.

Let's test the legalism reading against the text. A man comes up to Jesus and asks, 'How can I climb the ladder to heaven by doing things?' And we expect Jesus to reply, 'No! Stop trying to keep the law.' Instead, he says almost the opposite, and begins to recite key commands from the law! The man replies, 'I've kept these.' But instead of saying, 'That's quite enough doing of things, time to receive grace', Jesus says, 'Here's something else that you need to do.' How can the legalism reading make sense of this? Only perhaps by suggesting that Jesus is lying to the man, in order to test him. That really does start to create problems.

So what does Mr Nice Guy get wrong? The answer from Mark 10:21–22 seems pretty obvious: when given the choice between Jesus and his possessions, he chooses the latter. (Notice the 'for', **Linking Words tool**.) But how does this fit with the earlier discussion about his legal observance? We wondered whether it is significant that Jesus cites only six commandments, when every good Sunday school pupil knows that there are ten. The man appeared to score highly, but he's only completed half the exam paper. When it comes to 'no other gods before me' and 'don't make an idol', he fails catastrophically. His money has become his god. Mr Nice Guy's problem is not that he *tries* to be good, but that when it comes to the crunch, he fails to be good. His problem is not that he delights in God's law, but that he breaks God's law (compare Romans 2:23). In many ways, he is a nice bloke, but he comes to prove Jesus' statement that 'no one is good except God alone'.

The **Context tool** helps us to understand Mr Nice Guy's mistake in categories that are becoming very familiar. If we line up 10:21 against 8:34–35, the parallels are clear: 'If anyone would come after me, let him deny himself and take up his cross and follow me' is applied to this man as 'sell all you have and give to the poor . . . and come, follow me'. The promise that 'whoever loses his life . . . will save it' is applied to this man as 'you will have treasure in heaven'. Tragically, this man refuses to deny himself, and so he cannot be a disciple.

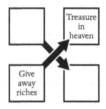

Impossible . . . but possible?

As the man walks off, Jesus offers his disciples a devastating analysis of what has gone wrong. The **Repetition tool** helps us feel the force of it: for a rich person to enter the kingdom of God is 'difficult' (v. 23), 'difficult' again (v. 24), harder than shenanigans with camels (v. 25), indeed, 'impossible' (v. 27). The **Tone and Feel tool** pushes us to consider not just what is being said, but *how* it is being said, and in this case, Jesus' teaching hits home by conjuring up mental images of unforgettable absurdity. Needles' eyes are small.[7] Threading them with fine cotton can be tricky, let alone with large mammals. And even among the large animals that Jesus could have chosen, camels are perhaps the least streamlined! In an attempt to illustrate this for the teenagers on camp, I (Tim) raided a friend's sewing kit and set off with a video camera into a field of pregnant cows . . .

Is Jesus targeting rich people in particular here? Yes and no. He opens the discussion with a reference to 'those who have wealth' (v. 23), and has warned already in his teaching about the thorn-like 'deceitfulness of riches' that chokes the seed of the gospel (4:19). But in the wider context, Jesus is just adding materialism to a much longer list of 'won't-deny-yourself' sins that exclude people from the kingdom: self-serving pride, failure to cut off limbs, cheap divorce, unwillingness to welcome children. In many ways, Mr Nice Guy had seemed our best hope so far. He was a nice guy! So when even he fails, the disciples ask with astonishment, 'Then who can be saved?' By the end of the paragraph, Jesus' verdict of 'impossible' seems to embrace everyone.

This is a good point at which to step back and take in the bigger picture. It's time for the **Author's Purpose tool**, as we try to understand why Mark included the various episodes that comprise this section. The episodes with the Pharisees and Mr Nice Guy are united by the theme of law-breaking, but what of severing limbs and welcoming children, and so on? Even at the outset, as we came up with a rough structure, the bookends had signalled one of the unifying themes: the first must be last. Jesus has made clear that denying yourself, taking up your cross and following him, in a sin-fighting, childlike, last-of-all way is *essential*. And yet, as we've gone through this part of Mark's Gospel in detail, a second theme has come to the fore: the first aren't good at being last. They keep failing. Indeed, it is *impossible*.

Essential but impossible? That's a scary combination.

But then comes something that doesn't quite seem to fit. When Peter says, 'See, we have left everything and followed you' (10:28), we assume that he has misunderstood. But Jesus does not contradict him. Indeed, at the start of the Gospel, Mark told us that Peter and his brother 'left their nets and followed [Jesus]' (1:18, anticipating the language of 8:34). The question is: how? If it is impossible for selfish human beings to deny themselves, take up their crosses and follow Jesus, how have Peter and the others managed to start along this road? It must fit into the 'all-things-are-possible-with-God' category (10:27), but that's all we are told at this stage. How God makes the impossible possible is the big unresolved question that we carry forward.

The section ends with yet another affirmation of the lose-life / save-life principle. As he has done previously, Jesus promises 'persecutions' now in exchange for 'eternal life' in the age to come. The new idea here is that some blessings are received *even in this life*. Indeed, Jesus promises a hundredfold compensation for anything that was lost. You can imagine v. 30 being a favourite among prosperity teachers – those who appear on satellite TV promising that God will boost your bank balance if you boost theirs. But a closer look reveals that Jesus can't mean that you will literally become a huge landowner, unless he also means that through some freaky biology, you will come to have a hundred mothers! Rather, he speaks of the wonderful blessing of church family: homes to be welcomed into, meals to be shared. We couldn't help but think of a certain Muslim convert at our church, disowned by his parents, but surrounded by Christian brothers and sisters, and announcing with a smile, 'This is my family.'

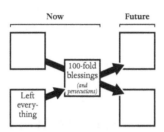

A king's ransom (10:32–52)

We've seen already that Mark structures chapters 8 – 10 around three predictions of Jesus' death. After each one comes teaching on how to follow in Jesus' steps, which the disciples consistently fail to do. We are now entering the third cycle. But to get the full cumulative impact, we need to read it in the light of the previous two.

DIG DEEPER: **Context tool**

Compare the three predictions of Jesus' death (8:31; 9:31; 10:32–34). What do they have in common? How is this third one ramped up in intensity relative to the others?
Compare the three exposés of the disciples following each death prediction. What do they have in common? How is this third one (10:35–45) ramped up relative to the others?

I (Andrew) know nothing about football, but, fed up with being excluded from the football chat in the office, I once asked my friend Sam (whose knowledge is encyclopaedic) for some stock phrases that I could insert into conversation: 'The problem with England is they've never had left-footed players', or 'Typical long-ball play from Stoke City'. Everyone was impressed at first, but they soon discovered that beneath the surface, I had no understanding whatsoever.

It seems that something similar is going on with the disciples here. They talk as though they have taken on board Jesus' teaching about his death and resurrection. They've picked up the vocabulary of future glory (v. 37), and when he asks if they are able to endure the necessary suffering on the way (that is what the reference to his cup and baptism means), they give a confident 'yes'. But Jesus' cross-examination quickly reveals that they have no understanding whatsoever. Their version of 'lose life to save life' is entirely self-serving (not so far removed from the Islamist doctrine of martyrdom in exchange for a virgin-stocked paradise). Jesus' version is all about love for others.

And so Jesus finds himself again having to repeat the first-last principle which had bookended the previous section: 'whoever would be great among you must be your servant, and whoever would be first among you must be slave of all' (vv. 43–44; compare 9:35; 10:31). It's the opposite of how 'those who are considered rulers of the Gentiles' behave (v. 42). But it is exactly how the Son of Man behaved (**Linking Words tool**, first half of v. 45).

St Helen's Bishopsgate, where we serve, is located slap bang in the middle of the City of London, dwarfed by towering skyscrapers with comedy names (the 'Gherkin', the 'Cheese-grater', the 'Walkie-Scorchie', etc.). Businesses in each of these buildings employ top executives on the kind of salaries that would make your eyes pop out. They also employ cleaning staff on close to the minimum wage. Can you even imagine a chief executive walking past a cleaner and stopping to say, 'You're looking a bit tired. Why don't you put your feet up and let me finish mopping the loos for you? Here are the keys to my Bentley so you can get home more easily. I'll take the bus'? Of course not. It would never happen. But let's escalate it a bit. Instead of the CEO of a global company, how about the Ruler of all creation? Instead of mopping the floor, how about if he gave up his life to death? Can you even imagine it?

Here is the extraordinary example set by the Son of Man. He came not to be served, as well he might have done, but to serve. He is first because he put himself last. And his followers must do the same.

But his followers haven't done the same. Not so far anyway. They keep getting it wrong. Jesus has patiently corrected them. But then they get it wrong again. More tuition in Jesus' Sunday school doesn't seem to fix it. If you plotted their performance on a graph against time, you'd be hard-pressed to discern even the shallowest upward trend. This is a problem, because as we've seen from 8:34 onwards, denying yourself, taking up your cross and following Jesus is not an optional extra. Whoever would save his life will lose it, Jesus had said. Yet so often, we shy away from self-sacrifice. If your hand causes you to sin, cut it off or face hell, Jesus had said. Yet so often, it does cause us to sin, and we take no action. Sell all you have and give to the poor, Jesus had said. Yet so often, we imagine that God will be impressed with the Mr Nice Guys among us and overlook our idolatry. We have as much chance of getting into the kingdom of heaven as the proverbial camel. The cross-shaped life is essential, but it is impossible.

Substitution and spiritual sight

Human beings can be quite creative when it comes to problem solving. We were amused to read of the Longxiang Bus Company in China, which decided to hang large bowls of water next to their drivers to discourage fast cornering; or Marah Land Zoo in Gaza, which responded to the deaths of two zebras by painting stripes on donkeys! But when it comes to the problem of our sin, Mark is about to unveil a solution that was beyond human ingenuity and full of the glory of God. We had a hint of it already earlier in the chapter: 'With man it is impossible, but not with God' (10:27). And here it comes. It's actually a double solution: substitution and spiritual sight.

The theme of substitution is dropped as a surprise bombshell at the end of v. 45. The verse began, as we saw above, by setting forth Jesus as an example of how the disciples should have lived. But the verse ends by describing his death as the solution for their failure to have lived like that: the Son of Man came 'to give his life as a ransom for many'.[1]

Thanks to Somalian pirates, among others, we are familiar with the idea of paying a 'ransom' to secure someone's freedom from a hostile power. But the **Vocabulary tool** prompts us to check the biblical meaning of the term. It is closely related to the word 'redeem' or 'redemption', and often looks back to God's great rescue of his people at the exodus. It is used there both in the sense of rescuing from the tyranny of Pharaoh (the Somali pirate dimension, see Exodus 6:6), and in the sense of paying a price *to God*, for someone whose life would otherwise be forfeit (see e.g. Exodus 13:11-16). The latter is closely connected to the Passover, on which more later. Having already noticed Mark's obsession with the exodus at the feeding of the 5,000, it seems sensible to let that colour our understanding of the ransom spoken of here: Jesus' death will accomplish a massive new exodus rescue.

The ultimate determiner of a word's meaning, however, is always the **Context tool**. The context of the sentence tells us that the ransom price is the life of Jesus, and that it is paid on behalf of many. The context of the wider section helps us to see why the cost of rescue is so high: Jesus had said that the penalty for failed discipleship was to lose your life and be thrown into hell (8:35; 9:43–49). James and John and the others have failed, and by rights they should die under God's judgment. But as their penal substitute, Jesus will give his life in exchange for theirs.

The theme of spiritual sight comes in the account of Bartimaeus, son of Timaeus (10:46–52). On the surface of things, he's a blind man who recognizes Jesus' authority and asks for his sight back. The **Context tool** persuades the careful reader that more is going on, because this is the second time we've seen a blind man being healed. Mark showed us that the first was not only about physical sight, but also about the supernatural enlightenment of Peter to recognize Jesus as the Christ. It came just in time, because we were really beginning to despair of the disciples ever grasping anything. But strangely, the miracle took part in two stages, with a blurry 'men-like-trees-walking' half-healed state. The second healing also comes at a moment when we as readers are exasperated at the disciples' lack of understanding of the cross-shaped life. If they have any spiritual vision, it's at best blurred, and further intervention by the spiritual optician is needed!

So, is this the point when Peter is finally converted? Or was that back in 8:29? Or is it not until later, after he has denied Jesus and the cock crows, and Jesus restores him? Or is it still later, when the Holy Spirit is given? Although conversion, with a definite before and after, is an important part of New Testament teaching (e.g. John 5:24; Acts 2:38–41; Ephesians 1:13), it doesn't seem to be Mark's intention to pinpoint a particular 'when'.[2] He wants to teach a more general lesson: believers never stand on their own two feet spiritually speaking; every step of the way, we are dependent on enlightenment from Jesus (compare Ephesians 1:18).

Together, substitution and spiritual sight fix the problem. Putting on a systematic theology hat, we might say that substitution addresses the problem from God's perspective, because otherwise he could not pardon sinners. And spiritual sight addresses the problem from our perspective, because otherwise we could not follow God. Neither solution would suffice by itself, and it's no surprise that in Scripture, we frequently find them together:

Changing us from the inside	Satisfying God's justice
'I will put my law within them, and I will write it on their hearts . . . they shall all know me' (Jeremiah 31:33–34).	'For I will forgive their iniquity, and I will remember their sin no more' (Jeremiah 31:34).
'Truly, truly, I say to you, unless one is born of water and the Spirit, he cannot enter the kingdom of God' (John 3:5).	'For God so loved the world, that he gave his only Son, that whoever believes in him should not perish but have eternal life' (John 3:16).
'[H]e saved us . . . by the washing of regeneration and renewal of the Holy Spirit' (Titus 3:5).	'. . . so that being justified by his grace we might become heirs' (Titus 3:7).

Before we close, there is more to learn from Bartimaeus than the fact that he receives physical sight, and thereby teaches us about spiritual sight. In various other ways, it seems that Mark holds him up as the model disciple, a prime candidate for the **Copycat tool**. (The point of the tool is that we don't make a role model out of any character we choose, but only those that *the author intends* to be thought of in this way.)

The **Repetition tool** highlights the model approach: 'Son of David, have mercy on me!' He knows who Jesus is ('Son of David' is a Messianic title; see 2 Samuel 7:12–13), and he knows what he needs from Jesus. The humility of his request is the more obvious when we realize that Jesus' question: 'What do you want me to do for you?' (Mark 10:51) is the very same as he asked James and John back in v. 36. They wanted glory. Bartimaeus wants to see.

The **Context tool** highlights the model response: 'immediately he recovered his sight and followed him on the way' (v. 52). At the beginning of this section of the Gospel, Jesus invited any who would come after him to 'deny himself and take up his cross and follow me'. In 10:21–22, a rich man declined to do so. Now a poor beggar gladly accepts, and sets off after Jesus along the road that leads to the cross. It's a road marked by self-denial, and serving others, and suffering persecution, and fighting sin. It's a road that leads to life.

Let's finally pull together all of the threads that have woven through this section. We've seen that the cross-shaped life is essential but impossible. We can't attain it, and our failure to attain it will shut us out of the kingdom. Wonderfully, Jesus brings a double solution. As our substitute, he offers his life as a ransom for ours. But he also opens our spiritual eyes, so that we might see the right way. Some are content to leave it there, as though the function of Jesus' moral teaching were *only* to expose our failure and cause us to throw ourselves on his mercy. But Mark doesn't leave it there. After hearing that God makes the impossible possible, we are told that Peter 'left everything' to follow Jesus. And after hearing of mercy shown to a blind beggar, we read that he 'followed him on the way'. Presumably, Bartimaeus' friends would begin to notice various changes in him: a new willingness to serve others, radical action whenever a hand or foot or eye caused him to sin, lifelong faithfulness to his wife (if he was married), a diminishing concern for material prosperity.[3]

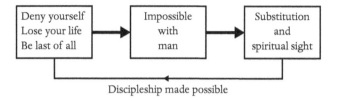

Discipleship made possible

Please don't mishear us. Mark isn't teaching that Jesus helps us to obey his commands, and that by our obedience, we merit eternal life. No! Eternal life comes to us as a gift because Jesus has paid our ransom. But as ransomed people, with our spiritual eyes opened, we are helped to obey Jesus' commands.

> Praise, my soul, the King of heaven;
> To His feet thy tribute bring;
> Ransomed, healed, restored, forgiven,
> Who like thee His praise should sing?
> Praise Him, praise Him,
> Praise the everlasting King.[4]

Roll out the red carpet (11:1–25)

The King arrives in Jerusalem . . . to save

At the time of writing, the last few years have been eventful ones for Her Majesty the Queen: the wedding of William and Kate; the Diamond Jubilee celebrations, in which she managed to look dignified boating down the Thames in miserable weather; her appearance as a Bond girl in the London Olympics opening ceremony (we laughed so much when she jumped out of the helicopter); the birth of her great-grandson, Prince George. As we reflect on the media coverage of the many royal processions – the images of crowds lining the streets, waving union jacks, shouting with excitement – we get something of a picture of what it must have looked like for King Jesus to arrive in Jerusalem.

But imagine how odd it would have been to read the description of the Royal Wedding, and find that over half of the column inches were taken up with a description of where the chauffeur picked up the Queen's Rolls-Royce. As we read Mark 11:1–11, the **Repetition tool** goes crazy with references to the acquisition of Jesus' transport: 'you will find a colt tied . . . And they . . . found a colt tied . . . "What are you doing, untying the colt?" . . . And they brought the colt to Jesus.'

Clearly, the author wants to draw our attention to this beast. But why? It's not immediately obvious to the reader why riding on a colt is so significant, and so we begin to wonder if there might be some relevant Old Testament background. Looking up 'colt' in the ESV on www.Biblegateway.com throws up three Old Testament references:

> Binding his foal to the vine
>   and his donkey's colt to the choice vine,
> he has washed his garments in wine
>   and his vesture in the blood of grapes.
> (Genesis 49:11)

> But a stupid man will get understanding
>   when a wild donkey's colt is born a man!
> (Job 11:12)

> Rejoice greatly, O daughter of Zion!
>   Shout aloud, O daughter of Jerusalem!
> Behold, your king is coming to you;
>   righteous and having salvation is he,
> humble and mounted on a donkey,
>   on a colt, the foal of a donkey.
> (Zechariah 9:9)

It is the task of the **Quotation/Allusion tool** to determine whether the author actually intended a cross-reference to any of these. We gave some criteria for assessing possible allusions when discussing the feeding of the 5,000. Suffice it to say that Genesis 49 and Job 11 totally fail to meet any of them. But when it comes to Zechariah, everything fits:

	Zechariah 9:9	**Mark 11:1–11**
The right character	'your king is coming'	'Blessed is the coming kingdom'
Approaching the right place	'Zion . . . Jerusalem'	'when they drew near to Jerusalem'
On the right animal	'mounted on a donkey, on a colt'	'they brought the colt to Jesus . . . and he sat on it'
With the right response	'Shout aloud'	'those who followed were shouting'

OK then. Mark wants us to notice the colt in order to point to some words written around 500 years beforehand. But why? The main point of Zechariah's prophecy was to tell us that God's King would come in humility to save. And that fits exactly with where we have got to in Mark – a King who came not to be served, but to serve and to give his life as a ransom for many (10:45). Indeed, the **Context tool** gives us even more reason to link back to the previous chapter. When we read that 'many spread their cloaks on the road' and were shouting about the 'coming kingdom of our father David' (11:8, 10), we can't help but think of Bartimaeus, who called Jesus 'Son of David' and threw off his cloak to follow him (10:47, 48, 50).

After the three predictions of Jesus' death and resurrection in chapters 8 – 10, we come to the final major section of this Gospel. We have arrived at our final destination on the map: all of the remaining action will take place in and around Jerusalem. And we've entered the final week in the diary: there are only a few days now before Jesus will be arrested and killed. The King arrives in Jerusalem . . . to save.

The King arrives in Jerusalem . . . to announce coming judgment

The verses that follow surprise people. They worry that Jesus loses his temper irrationally with a tree. They worry that he is horticulturally ignorant, unaware of the right time to harvest figs. If only they had learned how to use the **Structure tool!**

DIG DEEPER: **Structure tool**

Identify the three sections that make up 11:12–21. How do these three sections fit together? (Hint: remember a structural technique that Mark has used previously, for example, in 8:11–30.)

The structural feature that you've (hopefully) identified invites us to make comparisons. How is the condition of the fig tree a picture of the spiritual condition of the temple? How is the fate of the fig tree a picture of the final end of the temple?

The soppy Jesus of popular imagination, who cuddles lambs, wears a nightie and responds to evil only by being sad, doesn't fit well with 11:15–19. The historical facts are these: Jesus comes to the temple in Jerusalem and is angered at what he finds there. He flips tables full of coins. He kicks over chairs. He single-handedly brings trade to a standstill. But these violent actions are only a sign of the final destruction of the temple that would come a few years later.

The **Structure tool** has already helped us to understand something of what is wrong with the temple and what its end will be. But we can get to the same place using the

Quotation/Allusion tool. (It's a sure sign that you've locked on to the author's purpose when different features of the text converge on the same point.) Above the sound of clattering coins and squawking pigeons, we hear Jesus quote first from Isaiah 56:7 – 'My house shall be called a house of prayer for all the nations' (Mark 11:17) – explaining what the temple was supposed to be – but then from Jeremiah 7:11 – 'you have made it a den of robbers' – stating what it had become. It is when we explore the wider context in Jeremiah 7 that the specific lessons taught by the fig tree pop up again:

> Will you steal, murder, commit adultery, swear falsely, make offerings to Baal, and go after other gods that you have not known, and then come and stand before me in this house, which is called by my name, and say, 'We are delivered!' – only to go on doing all these abominations? Has this house, which is called by my name, become a den of robbers in your eyes? Behold, I myself have seen it, declares the LORD. Go now to my place that was in Shiloh, where I made my name dwell at first, and see what I did to it because of the evil of my people Israel . . . I will do to the house that is called by my name, and in which you trust, and to the place that I gave to you and to your fathers, as I did to Shiloh. (Jeremiah 7:9–14)

Looking up the original context of an Old Testament quotation always helps our understanding.[1] If we had read only 'den of robbers', we might have thought that Jesus' beef was specifically with the commercialization of temple worship and dodgy exchange rates at the moneychangers. In fact, the problem is broader. Jeremiah shows us that God is concerned not so much with what happens in the temple, but with what happens elsewhere in their lives. There is a mismatch between church on Sundays and the rest of the week. It's hypocrisy (cf. Mark 7:6), the religion of empty show, the leafy tree without fruit.

So what will happen to the temple? Jeremiah's hearers had thought it invincible, but he pointed them to the case of Shiloh, a previous place of worship that God had abandoned at a time of national apostasy (see 1 Samuel 4). In due course, the temple of his day was destroyed by the Babylonians. Jesus' hearers, then, should be clear on the historical precedent: corrupt temples end up as rubble, or, we might say, withered away to their roots. The King arrives in Jerusalem . . . to announce coming judgment.

Don't worry. Trust God

The next paragraph (Mark 11:21–25) seems to be a miscellany of new ideas – faith that moves mountains, answered prayer, the importance of forgiveness – but the **Context tool** reminds us that it all comes as Jesus' response to Peter's alarm at the withered fig tree. Why is Peter alarmed? Presumably, he has put two and two together and worked out that the temple's days are numbered, and worries, 'Can we still draw near to God, then?' (because the temple symbolized God's dwelling among his people); 'Can we still pray, then?' (because the temple was supposed to be the house of prayer for all nations); 'Can we still be forgiven, then?' (because the temple was where you offered sacrifices to atone for your sin).

Jesus answers 'yes' to all these questions. You can still pray and receive extraordinary answers to prayer.[2] You can still be forgiven, provided that you forgive others. But only if you believe – this is the emphasis highlighted by the **Repetition tool**: 'Have faith in God' (v. 22), '[he who] does not doubt in his heart' (putting it negatively) 'but believes' (v. 23), and 'believe that you have received it' (v. 24).

Gathering it all together, we can say that the King arrives in Jerusalem to save. But he also announces coming judgment. How should we respond to this news of judgment? By continuing to trust God. After all, he has a huge salvation plan underway.

The stone the builders rejected
(11:27 – 12:44)

While at Bible College, I (Andrew) wondered whether Jehovah's Witnesses have blacklists of addresses that rookie door-knockers should avoid. For example, the house in Farm Lane, Southgate, where our Doctrine Lecturer (who had a PhD on the Trinity) lived. Knock knock. Oops. Not your lucky day . . .

Jesus' address would have been blacklisted pretty quickly. In 11:27 – 12:44, we see him engage with a whole series of religious groups. Their attempts to tie him in theological knots fail so spectacularly that, after only a few tries, we are told that 'no one dared to ask him any more questions' (12:34).

It's usually best to start with the **Structure tool** to get our bearings. The different episodes are these:

- Conflict with the temple authorities concerning authority (11:27–33)
- Parable of the tenants (12:1–12)
- Conflict with the Pharisees and Herodians concerning taxes (12:13–17)
- Conflict with the Sadducees concerning the resurrection (12:18–27)

- A summary of the law, two warnings and an exemplary
  widow (12:28–44; we shall look at how to subdivide this
  further in due course)

The various conflicts have a lot in common, but the parable
sticks out. It seems that Mark has deliberately placed it in
the middle of the narrative as a commentary on everything
else.

The tenants (in the parable)

Summarizing something in your own words can be a useful
step towards understanding. Here's our attempt: The tenants
reject God and kill his Son; God rejects the tenants; God
vindicates his Son.

We get eight whole verses on 'The tenants reject God and
kill his Son', and they are designed to show the terrible
wrongness of it. Consider the detail even in the opening
sentence: 'A man planted a vineyard and put a fence around it
and dug a pit for the winepress and built a tower' (12:1). With
the **Quotation/Allusion tool** in hand, we realize that Mark is
deliberately referencing an Old Testament prophecy in which
God lovingly set up a vineyard, only to discover, to his horror,
that the fruit was inedible:

> Let me sing for my beloved
>> my love song concerning his vineyard:
> My beloved had a vineyard
>> on a very fertile hill.
> He dug it and cleared it of stones,
>> and planted it with choice vines;
> he built a watchtower in the midst of it,
>> and hewed out a wine vat in it;

and he looked for it to yield grapes,
> but it yielded wild grapes.

And now, O inhabitants of Jerusalem
> and men of Judah,
judge between me and my vineyard.
What more was there to do for my vineyard,
> that I have not done in it?
When I looked for it to yield grapes,
> why did it yield wild grapes?
(Isaiah 5:1–4)

But Mark changes Isaiah's metaphor to paint an even worse picture. This time it's not that the fruit is bad, but that it's withheld from the owner by violent means. The **Repetition tool** helps us to feel the shock:

> . . . he sent a servant . . . And they took him and beat him and sent him away empty-handed. Again he sent to them another servant, and they struck him on the head and treated him shamefully. And he sent another, and him they killed. And so with many others: some they beat, and some they killed.
> (Mark 12:2–5)

Finally, the owner sends his son. Remembering the **Tone and Feel tool**, ask yourself what is achieved by the extra details in v. 6: the son is 'beloved', and his proud father is sure that his son will be respected. Why are we told this? To show us that the owner is naive? Surely not. Rather, to show us, with considerable pathos, what the owner had every right to expect. His son *should* have been honoured. But instead, he is killed in an attempt to seize his inheritance. It is monstrously evil.

We have paused, rightly, to consider the emotional impact of these verses. But notice also their theological importance. Jesus explains his death in relation to his hearers' rejection of God the Father. Their opposition to him is merely the fullest expression of their hatred of the vineyard owner.

And so, Jesus asks, 'What will the owner of the vineyard do?' (v. 9). The genius of the parable is that we know the right answer even before Jesus tells us. (Isaiah's vineyard prophecy works the same way.) The tenants' crime has so outraged us, the readers, that we demand justice. Quite so, says Jesus; God 'will come and destroy the tenants and give the vineyard to others' (v. 9). The **Context tool** reminds us of the wineskins warning of 2:22 – as the Pharisees plot to destroy Jesus, they face their own destruction. Retribution is deserved. If we are squeamish about the language of vengeance in the Bible, it can only be that we have an inadequate grasp of the heinousness of the crime.

Jesus closes with a quotation from Psalm 118 that speaks of his final vindication: 'The stone that the builders rejected has become the cornerstone' (Mark 12:10). Imagine you walk past a building site one day. You overhear a group of builders on their tea break slagging off the architect's plans and cheering as two of their mates sling a large piece of masonry into a skip. But the next day, those builders are nowhere to be seen, and you notice a bunch of fresh faces continuing the work. And hang on a minute, what's that right at the foundation of the building? It's the stone from the skip! The architect has restored it to pride of place.

How can a rejected stone become a cornerstone if the rejection involves a murder? Surely a resurrection is implied. The **Context tool** helps, because we've been told repeatedly that three days after his rejection, Jesus will rise again (8:31; 9:31; 10:34). And having (of course) used the **Quotation/Allusion**

tool to check the original context of Psalm 118, we found further hints:

> I shall not die, but I shall live . . .
>> he has not given me over to death . . .
> The stone that the builders rejected
>> has become the cornerstone.
> (Psalm 118:17, 18, 22)

Tim once went along to a Kanye West gig and can't help but think of his number-one hit: 'N-now th-that that don't kill me, can only make me stronger.' But perhaps we can modify it slightly: 'N-now th-that that *does* kill me, can only make me stronger.' Jesus is unbeatable. Rejecting him will not succeed in overthrowing his position as Son and heir to the kingdom. All it will achieve is your own rejection.

The tenants (in the temple courts)

We said that the parable helps us understand the various conflicts in the temple courts. Each follows the same pattern: a group of religious leaders tries to trap Jesus by asking a tricksy question, but Jesus turns the tables with a devastating question of his own. As they try to reject the Son, they find themselves rejected.

Round One: Temple Authorities v. Jesus. The authorities win the toss, and are straight on the offensive: 'By what authority are you doing these things, or who gave you this authority to do them?' (11:28). It might seem a reasonable question, given the hullabaloo that Jesus has just caused with the money-changers and pigeon-sellers, except that Mark has already given users of the **Context tool** cause to suspect the questioners' motives: in 11:18 we were told that 'the chief priests and the scribes [i.e. the same people] . . . were seeking a way to destroy him'. This is a trap. If Jesus says his authority is from heaven, they will do him for blasphemy. If he says it's from earth, then what right did he have to smash up God's temple?

In a spectacular boomerang move (to mix the sporting metaphors!), Jesus asks them an equivalent question concerning the baptism of John: was it from heaven or from earth? They have the same two answers available, but Jesus has got them either way. (John of course had endorsed Jesus' ministry; **Context tool**, 1:2–8.) So they won't answer his question. And Jesus doesn't see why he should answer theirs. 1–0.

Notice the link to the parable. John was a prophet, one of the messengers sent by the owner of the vineyard to collect his due. But they refuse to acknowledge him, because they have no regard for the owner.

DIG DEEPER: 12:13–17, Pharisees and Herodians v. Jesus (Round Two)

In previous Dig Deeper exercises, we've given you a specific tool to work with. This time we're giving you a paragraph, for which you'll need various tools.

Perhaps use the **Structure tool** to subdivide the paragraph. Where are the tables turned?

Perhaps use the **Context tool** to consider the past form of Jesus' opponents (e.g. 3:6; 7:6).

Perhaps use the **Quotation/Allusion tool** to evaluate the cross-reference that some people make to Genesis 1:26. Are you persuaded? (Not all proposed allusions are legitimate!)

Perhaps use the **Context tool** again to consider how this episode fits with the parable.

Whatever conclusions you came to, we hope you'll agree that after Round Two, it's 2–0 to Jesus.

Round Three: Sadducees v. Jesus. The **Narrator's Comment tool** invites us to pause on 12:18. Mark tells us as an aside that Sadducees don't believe in the resurrection, so that we shall see their question about the resurrection (!) for what it is. (Tim is begging me not to include the corny joke, but I, Andrew, have control of the keyboard today, so here it is: they don't believe in life after death; that's why they are *sad, you see*? Hahahaha.) Their riddle is based on the law of Levirate marriage (see Deuteronomy 25:5) and runs to a whole paragraph. You can imagine them being enormously pleased with themselves for thinking it up. The punchline is so disingenuous: 'In the resurrection [which we don't believe in], when they rise again [which we don't think they will], whose wife will she be?'

The trouncing they receive is enjoyable to read, and worthy of the **Tone and Feel tool**. Jesus could have said straightaway, 'You're wrong', but instead asks, 'Is this not the reason that you are wrong?' (Mark 12:24). We love that. The fact that they are wrong is a given, and the only thing worth exploring is why. The answer: 'you know neither the Scriptures nor the power of God'. Ouch. Then a brief theological tutorial (God made promises to Abraham, Isaac and Jacob that weren't fulfilled in their lifetime, so either he's unfaithful – which is unthinkable – or they are going to rise again. Go figure).[1] And finally, a summary, in case they missed it first time round: 'You are quite wrong' (v. 27).

Notice again the link to the parable. If there is a resurrection, then not only are the Sadducees wrong, but, like the proverbial builders, they should watch out. Rejecting this stone, even by killing him, will not be the end of the story.

What does the **'So What?' tool** make of all this? Before we apply it to those who reject Jesus today, we need to remember that this speaks first and foremost about the specific group of people who killed Jesus. It's important that we know that their theological arguments were a sham, that they were driven not by the honest quest for truth, but by a deep-seated hostility to God. It's not naive to trust Jesus in the face of their rejection. The case against him collapses under cross-examination.

Loving God with everything or nothing

So far we've had the temple authorities, Pharisees, Herodians and Sadducees pitting their wits against Jesus in (unsuccessful) attempts to topple him. Now 'one of the scribes came up' (v. 28), and we expect him to do the same. But immediately, we notice that something is a bit different. First, he comes on his own. Secondly, in marked contrast to the others, there's nothing to suggest that his question is anything but genuine. Thirdly, he agrees with Jesus' answer: 'You are right, Teacher. You have truly said . . .' (v. 32). Finally, rather than being steamrollered by Jesus, he is told that he is 'not far from the kingdom of God' (v. 34). (Glass-half-empty people want to read 'not far' as 'still a long way to go', but the expression emphasizes closeness; Jesus' evaluation of him is certainly more positive than the 'You are quite wrong' of v. 27!)

It was these considerations that made us reluctant to lump this episode with those that have come before (despite the summary that comes in 12:34). This man is not quite like the other 'tenants', and a little work with the **Structure tool** suggested that he might begin a new mini-section:

One scribe commended (vv. 28–34)
    Scribes (plural) judged (vv. 35–37)
    Scribes (plural) judged (vv. 38–40)
One widow commended (vv. 41–44)

The friendly scribe and the widow are linked by the theme of wholehearted devotion to God. The scribe recognizes the need for it; the widow exemplifies it. He realizes that he should love God with '*all* the heart and with *all* the understanding and with *all* the strength' (**Repetition tool**, v. 33, italics added). She contributes to the offering box 'everything she had, *all* she had to live on' (v. 44, italics added).

The passages about the scribes (plural) are linked by the theme of judgment. In the first paragraph, Jesus challenges their idea that the Christ is the Son of David, which is odd, because that's exactly who he is! Bartimaeus even called him that, and we didn't object. So what's the problem? Simply that the scribes' view of David's son is too small. Psalm 110 (quoted) tells us that he is David's 'Lord', that is, someone greater than David, and that he will sit at the right hand of God the Father and destroy his enemies. The wider context of the psalm (**Quotation/Allusion tool**) abounds with images of vanquished foes. It is another clear warning to the rebellious scribes. In the second paragraph, Jesus focuses in on their behaviour. It is entirely self-serving: they 'like to' walk around in robes and to be acknowledged in public. It is devoid of spiritual reality: their beautifully crafted prayers are only 'for a pretence'. Again, Jesus finishes the paragraph with a warning of coming judgment (v. 40).

By sandwiching the judgment passages between the two references to wholehearted devotion, Mark invites us to make a comparison. The widow is everything that the scribes are not. If they were to give to charity, you can be sure that they would pose for the local newspaper with one of those over-sized cheques. Her two small copper coins would look pathetic on the front page, but then she's not giving them for the sake of appearances. She wants to honour God; they seek only to honour themselves. Mark draws the contrast even more sharply: she is a 'poor widow', and they 'devour widows' houses'. Her poverty funds their hypocrisy. We are surely intended to sympathize with Jesus' indignation at them. As with the parable of the tenants, a proper grasp of the heinousness of the crime helps us to see the appropriateness of the coming judgment.

The scribes (plural) also seem to contrast with the scribe (singular). Using the **Context tool**, we are reminded that they are the ones who are out of sorts with Jesus for his cleansing of the temple. He recognizes that to love God and to love one's neighbour is 'much more than all whole burnt offerings and sacrifices' (v. 33) – that is to say, the temple is worthless unless there is genuine faith.

Once again, it's time for the **'So What?' tool**. The primary purpose is still to explain why the fruitless temple was cursed and why the evil tenants were destroyed. And yet the meaning spills over into our own day, for the religion of the scribes is alive and well. Thinking back to Bible College days, I (Andrew) remember a reply I received from a particular religious trust to which I had applied for a book grant:

> We regret we are unable to provide you with assistance at this time. I have enclosed a photocopy of a page from *Crockford's* on How to Address the Clergy. Our members very much dislike being spoken of as though they came from North America.
> Yours sincerely . . .

Apparently, this was because I had written to 'The Reverend Smith', whereas the correct form of address in the UK is: 'The Reverend Mr Smith'. I am not even joking.

Love of religious titles, love of ostentatious religious clothing, love of invitations to exclusive dinners, love of correct liturgy, love of historic religious buildings, love of favourable media coverage, love of a substantial Twitter following, love of fat cheques in exchange for Christian services, love of a place on the platform at the big conventions, love of . . . well, really love of anything at the expense of love for God with all your heart, with all your soul, with all your mind, with all your strength, and love for your neighbour as yourself.

Beware. Judgment is coming.

The end of the world is nigh
(13:1–37)

Mark 13 is a famously difficult chapter. And so, when my colleague Philip joined my (Andrew's) Bible study to give feedback on my leadership skills, I decided to play a practical joke. Unbeknown to Philip, everyone was working to a carefully rehearsed script, as we gave a performance of the worst-ever Bible study on the phrase: 'the abomination of desolation' (13:14). I kicked off by asking, 'What is abominable *for you?*' (a postmodern approach, if ever there was one!), and everyone pitched in with suggestions. My own abomination was a jar of Nescafé, prompting a shouting match with Laura, who drinks the stuff: 'You're such a coffee snob!'; 'You wouldn't know decent coffee if it hit you in the face!' After a few similar contributions, we reached a climax with Dan and Brie, an American couple, who spoke passionately about their Republican politics: 'The United States used to be God's nation, but now it's become an Obamanation!' At this point, 'The Star-Spangled Banner' started playing through the hi-fi, and Philip realized he'd been had. (Philip, if you're reading this, thanks for being such a good sport.)

Before we consider some of the ways that this chapter has been understood, we wanted to set out a few ground rules that apply whenever Christians disagree:

1. The Bible must remain the highest authority. We settle disputes not by counting who has most professors on their side, or by asking which position 'feels right', but by looking together at the text of Scripture.

2. This means that we must have the humility to change our minds. There is cause for concern about the Christian who is *forever* changing his or her mind. But also about the Christian who will *never* do so.

3. It's a good discipline to try to put your opponent's argument in its strongest possible form before you critique it. If, for the sake of winning the debate, you caricature what they are saying (or if they themselves make a mess of saying it), there is a danger that you throw out an argument that later turns out to be true.

4. We shouldn't follow the Dodo bird, who tells Alice in Wonderland that 'everyone has won, and all must have prizes' – that is, that all possible readings are equally valid.[1] No, because the text has an author who wrote with a specific intention, there are right interpretations and wrong interpretations – or, at least (granting our limitations as readers), better interpretations and worse interpretations.

5. We must distinguish between issues of Christian orthodoxy, where we need to fall out with those who disagree (see e.g. Matthew 23:1–39; Romans 16:17–18; 2 John 9–11), and issues of disagreement between genuine Christians where we should show charity (e.g. Romans 14:1–12). We (Tim and Andrew) are privileged to work on a church staff team where there is absolute

unanimity on issues like the inerrancy of the Bible, the uniqueness of Christ and the nature of marriage, but we live with our differences on infant baptism, the role of the law of Moses and the meaning of Mark 13!

Much of the confusion stems from assigning bits of the passage to various times in history. Is a particular section about (a) Jesus' death and resurrection, (b) the destruction of the temple in AD 70, or (c) the Second Coming of Jesus at some still future date? In our Bible study group (when we did the *actual* Bible study, rather than the spoof one), we played the Mark 13 Game with a 'board' containing three date zones, and a series of 'counters' with pictures representing elements in the passage – a cock crowing, the sun going dark, angels gathering the elect from the four winds, and so on. Each person in turn was asked either to play a new counter, assigning it to one of the dates, or to move a counter that someone had already played, giving a reason for their move. Thus we debated back and forth.

(Warning: although we have called it a game, it actually involves the deepest digging of this whole book. We want to show you that careful reading and the Bible toolkit are all you need to evaluate even what the boffins say. Prepare to work up a sweat. Hopefully, in a few pages' time, you will be able to lean on your spade and smile. If you've 'hurt your back', and this sounds like too much hard work, then you can skip the stuff in the tables and still follow the argument. But we hope that most readers will at least have a go.)

If Peter Bolt, New Testament lecturer at Moore College in Sydney, had been playing, he would have placed all the counters on (a). Somewhat controversially, he has written that the 'abomination' refers to Jesus' death, and the 'coming of the Son of Man' refers to his resurrection. Here are some of his arguments.[2]

Feature of Mark 13	Proposed fulfilment at the cross/resurrection (Bolt)	Our response
Jesus tells the disciples three times to 'stay awake' (vv. 33, 35, 37).	At Gethsemane, three times the disciples fall asleep (14:37, 40, 41).	A valid observation – Bolt may be on to something.
Jesus foretells that the 'sun will be darkened' (v. 24).	At the crucifixion, there was 'darkness over the whole land' (15:33).	Again, a valid observation – Bolt may be on to something.
Jesus says his unknown coming could be 'in the evening, or at midnight, or when the cock crows, or in the morning' (v. 35).	The next couple of chapters of Mark's Gospel follow this timetable: evening (Last Supper), midnight (Gethsemane), cock crow (Peter's denial), morning (trial).	Hmm. The reference to the cock crow certainly makes the reader think of Peter's denial. But is this Jesus' coming? Also, Mark himself doesn't repeat the time markers of 'evening' or 'midnight', so the case is not as strong as it might sound.
The climactic moment of Jesus' discourse is his prediction that 'they will see the Son of Man coming in clouds with great power and glory' (v. 26).	The climactic moment of Jesus' trial is when he tells the high priest that 'you will see the Son of Man seated at the right hand of Power, and coming with the clouds of heaven' (14:62).	Hmm. It's interesting that Jesus *refers to* his coming in both contexts. But that's not the same thing as showing that the cross/resurrection *is* his coming.

Table continues overleaf . . .

Feature of Mark 13	Proposed fulfilment at the cross/ resurrection (Bolt)	Our response
Continued from previous page	This language is drawn from Daniel 7 (**Quotation/Allusion tool**), where the Son of Man *approaches* the Ancient of Days. Thus, it fits better with Jesus' resurrection and ascension *to* heaven, than with his coming *from* heaven.	Hmm. It's true that the Son of Man approaches the throne in Daniel 7. But according to the angels in Acts 1:11, Jesus will return *from* the throne in the same manner. The language of 'coming with clouds' could mean travel in either direction. If anything, the order in Mark 14:62 – 'seated . . . and coming' rather than 'coming and seated' – implies return.
Jesus warns that the disciples will be 'delivered over' (vv. 9, 11, 12).	The same verb is used ten times of Jesus being 'betrayed' or 'delivered over'.	Hmm. Bolt is right to notice a parallel between Jesus' fate and the fate of his disciples – it's the logic of 8:31–38 again. But they are distinct. Mark 13 is specific-ally about the *disciples'* persecution, and none of the specifics – beatings in synagogues, betrayal of children by parents, etc. – happened to Jesus.

Jesus speaks of an 'abomination of desolation' preceding his coming (v. 14).	The murder of God's Son is surely the most abominable thing we could imagine.	Argh! The **Context tool** raises some significant obstacles. Why does Bolt think that the cross is particularly bad for pregnant women (13:17)? And how does he make sense of Jesus' injunction to 'pray that it may not happen in winter' (v. 18), if Jesus was speaking of events that would take place within a week?
Jesus warns the disciples not to be led astray (vv. 20–21).	Judas goes astray by betraying Jesus, Peter by denying him.	Argh! The **Context tool** helps us to see that Jesus' warning specifically pertained to false christs, who don't feature obviously at the cross.

Most of us will want to place quite a few counters on (b). After all, it is Jesus' prediction that the temple would be reduced to a pile of rubble that kicks off the whole discussion. Jesus is asked to provide a 'sign when all these things are about to be accomplished' (13:4), and after warning of some things that are *not* significant – there will be various upheavals, but 'the end is not yet' (v. 7) – he names the 'abomination of desolation' as the signal that it's time for those in Judea to flee (v. 14). This is so geographically specific that it can only refer to the imminent fall of Jerusalem in AD 70. An ancient Jewish source that survives from around this time, Josephus' *Jewish War*, narrates awful details of the Roman siege, the terrible shortage of food, the massacre that took place when the walls were breached, the temple being set ablaze.[3] Jesus wasn't exaggerating when he said that there would be 'such tribulation as has not been from the beginning of the creation that God created until now, and never will be' (v. 19). As for the 'abomination' itself,[4] the **Quotation/Allusion tool** helps us, because in Daniel 9:27, 11:31 and 12:11, the same phrase is linked with prophecies about the profaning of the temple sanctuary and the end of temple sacrifices. This was partially fulfilled in 167 BC when Antiochus Epiphanes IV marched his armies on Jerusalem, set up an altar to Zeus on top of the altar of burnt offering, and sacrificed a pig. It seems that something similar happened in AD 67/68 when the Zealots took control of the temple, and for a laugh consecrated their own high priest, provoking a public outcry and fighting within the temple courts. This was the sign that the temple, and the city, would soon fall. The point of these verses, then, is not to get us searching out our own abominations, but specifically to preserve the Christian church in Judea in the middle of the first century.

It's when we read of stars falling from heaven and angels gathering up Christians for salvation (vv. 24–27) that we want to start putting counters on (c). Although the chapter began by Jesus answering the disciples' question about the end of the temple, now he seems to be talking about an even bigger event – his Second Coming and final judgment. That is, unless we follow R. T. France in his influential commentary. (N. T. Wright, former Bishop of Durham, goes for something similar.) France thinks that vv. 24–27 belong at (b) too, and that the 'Son of Man coming' refers to his judgment on Jerusalem in AD 70. Let's consider some of his arguments (see table on pp. 172–176).[5]

Lean back on your spade! We're now in a position to draw things together.

In the Mark 13 Game, counters have been played in all three game zones. Some of the moves have been bold, to say the least. The winning board, in our view, alternates between (b) and (c). Jesus speaks of judgment on the temple (vv. 1–23), then of his Second Coming to judge the whole world (vv. 24–27), next of his judgment on the temple within the disciples' lifetime (vv. 28–31), and then of his Second Coming to judge the whole world (vv. 32–37). Why switch back and forth like this? Because, just as a fig tree in leaf points to the nearness of summer, so the fall of Jerusalem in AD 70 tells us that the final judgment is around the corner.

For twenty-first-century readers, this is extremely important. This whole section of the Gospel has been about judgment – a withered fig tree, violently overturned tables, the destruction of wicked tenants, the promise of a pile of rubble where a temple once stood – but all of that judgment now lies in the past. That doesn't make it irrelevant, of course. The end of the temple has ushered in a whole new way of relating to God, with answered prayer and forgiven sins made possible through Jesus (11:21–25). The rebellion of the Jewish tenants has resulted in the inclusion of Gentiles in the vineyard (12:9).

Feature of Mark 13	Proposed fulfilment at AD 70 (France)	Our response
'In those days, after that tribulation' (v. 24).	It sounds like the 'tribulation' and the 'coming' happen at roughly the same time in history. This fits well if the 'tribulation' is the siege of the city and the 'coming' is the fall of the temple soon afterwards.	A fair point, though the timescale is not specified. Jesus could simply be saying that he will not return until some time after the fall of Jerusalem.
Jesus speaks of the darkening of the sun and moon, and the falling of stars from heaven (vv. 24–25).	Those who assume a literal fulfilment to Jesus' prophecy – the sun actually stopping burning hydrogen etc. – need to pick up the **Genre tool** and think again. This language of cosmic upheaval is drawn from Isaiah 13:10, where it refers *figuratively* to the overthrow of Babylon; the imagery of falling stars conveys only the scale of political change. It is appropriate vocabulary for Jesus to use for the fall of Jerusalem in AD 70.	Hmm. The **Quotation/Allusion tool** prompts us to check the original context of Isaiah 13:10, and we discover that even as the prophet describes (yes, in metaphorical terms) the fall of Babylon, he has in mind God's judgment on the whole earth. This is clear from the very next verse ('I will punish *the world* for its evil', v. 11), but also from the way in which the larger section of Isaiah's prophecy reaches a climax (24:21–23).[6] Jesus' vocabulary could refer to the fall of Jerusalem, but would be equally appropriate to describe his Second Coming.

'They will see the Son of Man coming in clouds with great power and glory' (v. 26).	This language is drawn from Daniel 7 (**Quotation/Allusion tool**), where the Son of Man *approaches* the Ancient of Days. Thus it better fits with Jesus' resurrection and ascension *to* heaven than with his coming *from* heaven. The context is a court of judgment (Daniel 7:10, 22, 26). We 'see' evidence of Jesus' heavenly enthronement on earth as Jerusalem is judged in AD 70.	Hmm. On Jesus' direction of travel, see our response to Bolt, above. We don't know whether he is coming or going, to coin a phrase! As for the context of judgment, this applies equally well to AD 70 or the Second Coming. The idea of Jesus being 'seen' in AD 70 seems a bit of a fudge: the various false christs ('Look, there he is!', v. 21) were presumably visible in person, and the more obvious contrast is with Jesus' appearance at the end of history, when we shall see him face to face.

Table continues overleaf . . .

Feature of Mark 13	Proposed fulfilment at AD 70 (France)	Our response
'And then he will send out the angels and gather his elect from the four winds, from the ends of the earth to the ends of heaven' (v. 27).	Jesus is referring to the church's mission to the Gentiles, following his judgment on Jerusalem in AD 70, and not to the final judgment. It may be that 'angels' should be translated simply as 'messengers' (**Vocabulary tool**); if they are heavenly beings, then they must be assisting the church in its evangelistic role.	Hmm. At first glance, France's suggestion seems to have the support of the **Context tool**: Jesus promised in 12:1–12 that God would 'destroy' those Jews who had rejected him (AD 70?) and 'give the vineyard to others'. And yet we know that the Gentile mission was underway long before AD 70 (see Romans 11 or the book of Acts). Also, 13:10 insists that the gospel must be preached to all nations 'first', not *after* the cataclysmic coming. As for the fancy footwork with the **Vocabulary tool**, 'angel' *can* mean messenger (e.g. Mark 1:2), but clearly refers to heavenly beings in the immediate context, 13:32. Do the angels gather evangelistically? Mission is usually described as sending out; the gathering-in image more naturally refers to the final judgment.[7]

'From the fig tree learn its lesson: as soon as its branch becomes tender and puts out its leaves, you know that summer is near. So also, when you see these things taking place, you know that he is near, at the very gates. Truly, I say to you, this generation will not pass away until all these things take place' (vv. 28–30).	Verse 30 is the 'single most embarrassing feature of chapter 13 for traditional Christian interpretation' because Jesus did not return within the lifetime of his first hearers. However, if he has been referring all along to the destruction of the temple in AD 70, then the difficulty disappears. In the illustration of the fig tree, the 'tender branches' correspond to the abomination of desolation that precedes the coming 'summer' of AD 70.	Hmm. We agree that the phrase 'all these things' in v. 30 must refer to the fall of Jerusalem. But we don't get why France thinks that the coming of Jesus must be included within 'these things'. Using the **Context tool**, we discover that the same phrase in v. 29 refers not to Jesus' coming, but to something that happens *beforehand*, signifying that he is near. This makes sense if the fall of Jerusalem – within the disciples' generation – foreshadows an even greater judgment to come. If so, the 'tender branches' of the fig tree are the events of AD 70 that precede the 'summer' of the Second Coming.

Table continues overleaf . . .

Feature of Mark 13	Proposed fulfilment at AD 70 (France)	Our response
'But concerning that day or that hour, no one knows' (v. 32).	There is a contrast between 'those days' (plural) of v. 24 and 'that day' (singular) of v. 32. The former is known (v. 29), the latter unknown. This means they can't be about the same event, so if v. 32 refers to Jesus' final return, then vv. 24–27 must be a different 'coming', i.e. the destruction of the temple in AD 70.	Hmm. Why does France force a contrast with v. 24, when it's more natural to read the 'But' of v. 32 against the background of the immediately preceding verses? As for the alleged difference in know-ability, why can't v. 29 mean: 'you know it will happen', and v. 32 add: 'you don't know exactly [in day or hour terms] when'? Finally, is the phrase, 'that hour', really sufficient to introduce a brand new topic out of the blue? It makes much more sense if Mark is *resuming* discussion of the Second Coming, which he has already introduced back in vv. 24–27.

Nonetheless, we might think that the urgency of chapter 13 belongs to a past age. No need to keep an eye out for abominations any more. No need to flee to the mountains at short notice. Judgment is done and dusted, isn't it? Absolutely not! The events of AD 70 point forward to an even greater judgment to come, when Jesus will destroy his enemies and send out his angels to gather his people safely to himself.

If anything, the chapter speaks even more powerfully to us today than it did to Mark's first readers in the 50s or 60s of the first century. Jesus had announced two dates for the diary, and we can look back in our history books and see that he was right about the first. He wasn't bluffing. Terrible judgment really did fall on Jerusalem. And so we can be sure about the second: terrible judgment really will fall upon the whole earth. The 'So What?' tool goes hand in hand with the Repetition tool in telling us how to respond: 'Be on guard, keep awake' (13:33); 'stay awake' (v. 35); 'Stay awake' (v. 37).

Because we don't know when Jesus will return, we don't write it in our diary. And because we don't write it in our diary, we forget that it's important. It gets swamped by things like 'Mum's birthday' and 'tenpin bowling with youth group' and 'project deadline'. Here's a suggestion. Why not write it in your diary every day? If you use Outlook or Google Calendar, make it a recurring event: 'Jesus may return?' Keep it always in mind. Be continually ready for the interruption. Stay awake.

Even though 13:5–13 seems primarily to be about the lead-up to AD 70, a few of the applications given there help us to flesh out the concept of 'staying awake'. First, we must beware of false teachers who come in Jesus' name. Chillingly, Jesus anticipates their success – 'they will lead many astray' (v. 6). And so we must be on guard. Secondly, we must be prepared to testify to the gospel, even when that brings persecution from the authorities (vv. 9–11), or even our families

(v. 12). In the first instance, Jesus is talking specifically to his apostles (**'Who Am I?' tool**), and we can be grateful for the way that the Holy Spirit strengthened them to spread the gospel, despite being hauled before councils (e.g. Acts 4:5–31), beatings (e.g. Acts 5:40–42) and martyrdoms (e.g. Acts 7:54–60; 12:2). But there must also be a wider application, because Jesus speaks for the need of the gospel to go to all nations (Mark 13:10). We must continue to speak of him, come what may. And 'the one who endures to the end will be saved' (v. 13).

Stay awake.

Stay awake.

Stay awake.

Adored and betrayed (14:1–25)

We have probably all been to unusual dinner parties. Andrew remembers the 'murder mystery dinner' where he turned up in character as a corrupt casino owner and freaked out his hosts' lodger. Tim remembers the student dinner party in Bristol where almost everyone else was in their pyjamas. There were others where someone dropped the cake. Or where someone said something they ought not to have said. There were the funny ones. The awkward ones. The food-poisoning ones. In this chapter of Mark, however, we read about two of the most important (and most unusual) dinner parties in history. At the first, someone smashes a jar of perfume worth more than £22,000.[1] At the second, the host announces that his guests are eating his own flesh. What on earth does all this mean?

Jesus' death forces us to take sides

We begin, as usual, with the **Structure tool**, and we discover immediately that the passage divides into two:

'two days before the Passover and the Feast of Unleavened Bread' (v. 1).

Dinner party 1: Perfume

'on the first day of Unleavened Bread, when they sacrificed the Passover lamb' (v. 12).

Dinner party 2: Passover

Mark gives us both dinners side by side, introduced by near-identical date formulae. Clearly, he intends a comparison. This becomes even more obvious when we realize that v. 3 and v. 18, within the two dinner party narratives, stand in direct contrast. Both begin with the words: 'As he was / they were reclining at table . . .' but they end very differently. Have a look and see what we mean. Did you get it? (We've always thought that the ESV lacked a 'the' before 'table', but it works if you give Mark a Yorkshire accent.)

The same contrast that we've just pointed out *between* the episodes is also made *within* the first episode. **Structure tool** still in hand, we zoom in on vv. 1–11 and discover a sandwich:

'the chief priests and the scribes were seeking how to arrest him by stealth and kill him' (v. 1).

A woman shows amazing devotion to Jesus (vv. 3–9).

'Then Judas Iscariot . . . went to the chief priests in order to betray [Jesus] to them' (v. 10).

So then, Mark sets up the whole chapter to showcase the difference between Judas and an unnamed woman. Judas betrays Jesus, while she adores him.

Let's consider the woman first. Her actions are so lavish that those who witness them are outraged. To be fair, we would react in the same way if we saw someone blowing a huge sum of money in a just-for-the-sake-of-it gesture. It would be like pushing your car off a cliff, tied up in red ribbon, just to send the video to someone you love. Or going to the bank, taking out your entire life savings in £50 notes, and setting light to the lot to keep someone warm. It's wastefully, *offensively* affectionate. It's almost sectionable. And yet it earns Jesus' commendation. He calls it beautiful. It's a story, he says, that will be retold throughout the world (he was right). The clue to why her seemingly crazy actions are actually spot on comes in v. 8. She has anointed Jesus' body for burial. We speculate in vain as to whether she herself realized this. Perhaps she only knew that she loved him, and it was Jesus who decided to infuse her actions with this theological significance. Either way, the point for Mark's readers is clear: Jesus' death is extraordinarily valuable.

With horrid irony, we might say that Judas also finds Jesus' death 'valuable': the subject of money, first introduced to measure the cost of the woman's sacrifice, recurs in v. 11 to highlight the profits of his treachery. But his gain will only be temporary: 'woe to that man by whom the Son of Man is betrayed! It would have been better for that man if he had not been born' (v. 21).

The extended contrast between Judas and the woman, and particularly the way that Jesus singles her out for commendation and him for condemnation, is our cue to reach for the **Copycat tool**. It works positively: Be like her! And negatively: Don't be like him! The positive application has teeth, because, if we're honest, we often feel fairly ambivalent towards Jesus and his death. Reading about her outlandish, just-for-the-sake-of-it actions wakes us up to our relative indifference, and it's significant that Mark challenges us with a £22,000 gesture of adoration just before we start reading about the events of Good Friday. But what about the negative example? Does Mark really want us to compare ourselves with Judas? Isn't he a one-off super-baddie, in his own special category of evil? Time for you to do some further digging.

DIG DEEPER: **Repetition tool**

What phrase is used repeatedly to describe Judas Iscariot in vv. 10, 20, 43?
How do vv. 18–19 repeat the same idea, albeit in different words?
What is the significance of Mark identifying Judas in this way?
How does this help us to take Judas more seriously as a negative example?

Jesus' death was a planned sacrifice to save us

Even as we see the plot against Jesus taking shape, Mark is keen to emphasize that Jesus is in total control of events:

- Consider Jesus' instructions concerning the preparations for Passover. He predicts a specific encounter with a specific man (carrying a jar of water), who leads them to a specific house where they have a specific conversation and are shown to a specific room. We got déjà vu (aka we used the **Context tool**) as we remembered the specific colt tied to a specific door back in 11:1–7. Jesus has everything meticulously planned.
- Consider Jesus' announcement of Judas' betrayal before it happens in v. 18. Actually, he foretold the same thing way back in 9:31 and 10:33 (made even clearer when, using the **Translations tool**, we discover that the phrase 'handed over' is identical to 'betrayed').

- Consider Jesus' insight that, even as Judas performs his evil deed, God's will is done and Scripture is fulfilled. This juxtaposition of God's sovereignty and human responsibility for sin is typical in Scripture, especially in relation to Jesus' death (e.g. Acts 2:23; 4:25–28; 13:27).

Muhammad died in Medina at the age of sixty-two or sixty-three in the arms of his wife Aisha. He was by then a wealthy man, and ruler of Arabia, thanks to his successful military conquests. The Buddha, according to legend, died at the age of eighty. Mao Zedong, founder of Communist China, died at the age of eighty-two, having suffered two major heart attacks, linked to his heavy smoking. By contrast, Jesus was a young man when he died, still in his thirties. And he *chose* to die.

Why on earth would Jesus choose to die? One of the places where he spells out the answer is 10:45. But there's another answer here, if we keep digging.

The **Repetition tool** reveals an emphasis on the Passover throughout the passage (14:1, 12, 14 and 16), and it's during the course of the traditional Passover meal that Jesus made his famous announcement: 'this is my body' (v. 22). It's a very strange thing to say, and you can imagine the disciples stopping mid-mouthful in alarm – compare your reaction if, halfway through Christmas dinner, your mother said of the turkey, 'Hope it's tender. It's my leg.' To understand what Jesus means, we need to use the **Genre tool** (to appreciate that Jesus is speaking figuratively and not literally) and the **Quotation/Allusion tool** (to appreciate what the symbolism means).

It's unfortunate, incidentally, that the Roman Catholic Church has got into a real mess with v. 22 as a result of *not* using these tools (and, perhaps, failing to read quite a lot of the rest of the Bible). According to the doctrine of transubstantiation, as the priest says certain magic words during

Mass, the bread literally becomes Jesus' body, while maintaining the so-called 'accidents' (i.e. physical appearance) of an ordinary piece of bread. I (Andrew) remember seeing an art exhibit in the Tate Modern that exposes this for the absurdity that it is. *An Oak Tree* by Michael Craig-Martin (1973) consists of a glass of water on a shelf with the following text alongside:

> Q. To begin with, could you describe this work?
> A. Yes, of course. What I've done is change a glass of water into a full-grown oak tree without altering the accidents of the glass of water.
> Q. The accidents?
> A. Yes. The colour, feel, weight, size.
> [. . .]
> Q. It looks like a glass of water.
> A. Of course it does. I didn't change its appearance. But it's not a glass of water, it's an oak tree.
> [. . .]
> Q. It seems to me that you are claiming to have worked a miracle. Isn't that the case?
> A. I'm flattered that you think so.[2]

So, what does Jesus mean by the language of 'my body'? If you've read the story of the original Passover in Exodus 12, then it should be immediately clear to you (and if you haven't, now is a good time to turn there in your Bible). In a final act of judgment against Egypt, God's angel was coming at midnight to strike down every firstborn son. God promised to spare his people only if they followed some very specific instructions: they were to kill a lamb, paint its blood on their doorposts and sit down to a roast dinner. 'And when I see the blood,' God had said, 'I will pass over you, and no plague will befall you to destroy you' (Exodus 12:13). Hence, it became known as the Passover, and was commemorated every year.

There was nothing unusual about Jesus sitting down with his disciples to celebrate this festival; they were doing what every Jewish family had done for centuries. But when Jesus spoke those words, 'This is my body', he spoke of a dramatic fulfilment. By identifying himself with the lamb, he was explaining that his death would be the means by which his people would escape God's judgment. If we trust in Jesus' sacrifice for our sins, he will pass over us on the day of his wrath.

This is, of course, not the first time that Mark has taken us back to the book of Exodus to explain Jesus' mission against the backdrop of the biggest rescue of the Old Testament. Remember the wilderness in 1:1-15. Remember the hard hearts of 3:5. Remember the 'manna from heaven' and 'crossing of the Red Sea' in 6:31-52. Remember the ransom of 10:45. There's one more allusion, as Jesus speaks of 'my blood of the covenant, which is poured out for many' (14:24).[3] This refers back to Exodus 24, where Moses sprinkled the Israelites with blood to seal the special relationship he was making with them; having rescued them, they belonged to him. But Jesus also points forward: 'Truly, I say to you, I will not drink again of the fruit of the vine until that day when I drink it new in the kingdom of God' (v. 25). If we trust in Jesus, then we belong to him and will meet him at a final dinner party, a heavenly banquet.

This is why Jesus planned to die. This is why it was written of him. This is why £22,000 of perfume is, if anything, a rather small gesture.

> Were the whole realm of nature mine,
> That were an offering far too small;
> Love so amazing, so divine,
> Demands my soul, my life, my all.[4]

 # The cock crows twice (14:26–72)

Early on in Shakespeare's famous Scottish play, Macbeth tells us that 'false face must hide what the false heart doth know'.[1] In this short phrase, he manages to encapsulate the essence of the play. Having murdered King Duncan in a bid for power, Macbeth and his wife attempt, with increasing desperation, to cover it up – 'false face must hide' – but in the end, their greatest enemy is not so much Macduff, who seeks to avenge their crimes, but their own tortured consciences – 'what the false heart doth know'. (All of this is courtesy of an English teacher friend, by the way; we were both pretty mediocre at Shakespeare at school.)

With similar literary skill, Mark manages to encapsulate the themes of a whole section in a single statement:

> And Jesus said to them, 'You will all fall away, for it is written,
> "I will strike the shepherd, and the sheep will be scattered."'
> (14:27)

There are two interrelated ideas here: first, that the disciples will abandon Jesus; secondly, that God will strike him. Let's consider them in turn.

The disciples abandon Jesus

It's been an unsettling evening for the twelve. Earlier, Jesus had said that one of them would betray him; now, he says that they will all fall away. Earlier, they were sad and confused; now, they are indignant: 'What do you mean, I'll abandon you, Jesus? Never! You can count on me! I'd sooner die than let you down!' Although all are full of the same bravado (v. 31), Mark focuses our attention on Peter. Even on first reading, experienced **Structure tool** users will have spotted the bookends: the whole section is framed by the promise of his betrayal (v. 30) and its tragic fulfilment (v. 72).

It begins, though, in Gethsemane (vv. 32–42). Jesus is full of distress as he contemplates the death he is about to die, and he asks his three closest friends to stay awake with him through the night. When he finds that they have dozed off, he is clearly upset: 'Simon, are you asleep? Could you not watch one hour?' Then, significantly, he cautions them to pray not simply against tiredness, but against temptation: there is a spiritual battle going on. Despite the warning, they fall asleep again. When Jesus rouses them the second time, they are ashamed and don't know what to say. But they still manage to get a bit more shut-eye before the betrayer arrives. Jesus is looking very alone. The close friends who had promised that they'd stand by him are not even there to offer comfort during his sleepless night.

Then, as Jesus is led away by an armed mob, 'they all left him and fled' (v. 50). For emphasis, Mark includes the story of a man who is so desperate to get away that he prefers the shame of public nakedness to the danger of standing by his Lord (vv. 51–52). But why? Is it simply cowardice? We might have said so, if not for the matter of the severed ear (v. 47): moments before, the disciples had been willing to risk their lives to fight for Jesus' freedom. So why do they run *now*? What's changed?

The key lies in Jesus' words to his captors: 'let the Scriptures be fulfilled' (v. 49). It seems that this is when the disciples finally 'do the math' (as Hollywood puts it) and realize that Jesus really does intend to die. He's told them many times, of course, but somehow it didn't compute. The Passover lamb must be sacrificed, he had said; the Shepherd must be struck. But only now, as he hands himself over to his captors without a struggle, do they understand that these prophecies describe what is actually about to happen to him. And so they flee.

In fleeing, they too fulfil Scripture. Perhaps you instinctively used the **Linking Words tool** when we quoted v. 27 above, but if not, then now is the time. 'You will all fall away, $\overleftarrow{for}$ . . .' Scripture foretells not only his striking, but also their scattering.

The final act in the tale of the disciples' abandonment of Jesus is the most poignant. The reader is given a flicker of hope in v. 54: 'Peter had followed him' (the **Context tool** reminds us of the significance of that particular phrase from 8:34). But then we continue the sentence – 'at a distance'. He's in two minds. Will he be the exception who sticks with Jesus – 'Even though they all fall away, I will not' (v. 29)? Or will Peter desert him too?

In the next few verses, Mark sets up a contrast between Jesus and Peter. In a sense, both are standing trial, but while Jesus is calm and composed before the high priest and the whole Council (vv. 55–65), Peter cracks under cross-examination from 'one of the servant girls of the high priest' (vv. 66–72). The **Tone and Feel tool** reminds us to consider the way in which events are retold, and here the action is slowed down. We hear Peter's first denial. Then the cock crows, *cock-a-doodle-doooooo*. It's a warning sign for him. Surely he will remember Jesus' words, and summon the courage to stand firm? But we read of a second denial. And a third. And then, right on cue, that fateful sound fills the air, *cock-a-doodle-doooooo*. This time Peter registers it, and remembers, and weeps (v. 72). We find this all the more moving when we consider that Peter was one of Mark's key witnesses as he compiled the Gospel.[2] Imagine him sitting there, recounting the events of that night: 'And then Mark, that's when the cock crowed the first time. But I kept on. I didn't just deny knowing him; I cursed; I swore. You'd better put that in too . . .'

It is an ugly series of events, as far as the disciples are concerned. As Jesus heads resolutely towards his death, they sleep and flee and deny. A final use of the **Context tool** helps us to see just how serious this is. Jesus had called each of them to 'deny himself and take up his cross and follow me' (8:34). But Peter doesn't deny himself; he denies Jesus (it is the same word in the original). He's chosen to save his life now, and we know that 'whoever would save his life will lose it' (8:35). He is ashamed of Jesus, and we have been told that 'whoever is ashamed of me and of my words in this adulterous and sinful generation, of him will the Son of Man also be ashamed when he comes . . .' (8:38). Consider the terrible danger that Peter and the others are in. They are in desperate need of rescue.

God will strike Jesus

Although we've mentioned v. 27 several times already, we've not yet done the responsible thing and used the **Quotation/Allusion tool**. Here is the original context:

'Awake, O sword, against my shepherd,
 against the man who stands next to me,'
  declares the LORD of hosts.
'Strike the shepherd, and the sheep will be scattered.'
(Zechariah 13:7)

Ultimately, it is not the chief priests or the Roman soldiers who strike Jesus, but God himself. If this were a new idea, it might baffle us, but Mark has already laid the groundwork. We know already that Jesus will 'give his life as a ransom for many' (10:45). We know already that, like the Passover lamb, he will die as a substitute for God's people, to avert God's wrath against them (14:22–25). Here we have the same idea, but with extraordinarily vivid imagery. God commands that his sword be awoken against Jesus. Divine judgment must fall on him.[3]

Jesus' awareness that he will soon face God's wrath on our behalf explains his anguish in the garden of Gethsemane. It's a scene unlike any other in the Gospel. If you were to summarize Jesus' attitude to danger so far, you would say he was Mr Calm and Collected. When faced with a life-threatening storm, he slept on a cushion. When faced with a legion of demons, he dispatched them into a herd of pigs without raising a sweat. But here, in the garden, Mr Calm and Collected is 'greatly distressed and troubled' and 'very sorrowful, even to death' (vv. 33–34). In a unique role-reversal, he seems to want to lean on his friends for support. What is it that so disturbs him? To understand his reference to 'this cup' (v. 36), we once again need the **Quotation/Allusion tool.**

Several of the Old Testament prophets use the imagery of drinking a cup of wrath to portray the terror of God's judgment. We find this in Isaiah 51:17–23, Jeremiah 25:15–29, Ezekiel 23:31–34 and Habakkuk 2:15–16. Jesus presumably had all these texts turning over in his mind. We hope that you might take the time to read them all, but here's Jeremiah's contribution:

> Thus the LORD, the God of Israel, said to me: 'Take from my hand this cup of the wine of wrath, and make all the nations to whom I send you drink it. They shall drink and stagger and be crazed because of the sword that I am sending among them.'

So I took the cup from the LORD's hand, and made all the nations to whom the LORD sent me drink it: Jerusalem and the cities of Judah, its kings and officials, to make them a desolation and a waste, a hissing and a curse, as at this day . . .

'Then you shall say to them, "Thus says the LORD of hosts, the God of Israel: Drink, be drunk and vomit, fall and rise no more, because of the sword that I am sending among you." '

(Jeremiah 25:15–18, 27)

Jesus' prayer in Mark 14:36 is remarkable. He is full of trepidation at what lies ahead, yet he is fully committed to going through with it. If we read, 'not what I will but what you will', as expressing a conflict between Jesus and his Father, then we have completely misunderstood the point. Rather, the tension is *within Jesus*, an internal battle between his strong feelings of anguish and his even stronger determination to obey. Deep down, he wants to do what his Father wants him to do. He wills his Father's will.

Jesus emerges resolute from his time of prayer. He allows himself to be arrested without struggle. He refuses to defend himself in court, even as the prosecution case collapses. The **Repetition tool** exposes the sham trial for what it is: 'many bore false witness . . . but their testimony did not agree'; 'some stood up and bore false witness . . . Yet even about this their testimony did not agree' (vv. 56–59). How, then, do they arrive at a guilty verdict? Jesus hands it to them (v. 62). Mark portrays him as the one in total control even of his own conviction.

Putting it all together

We've dealt with this chapter under two headings, tracing through the two main themes. But if we take up the **Structure tool**, it's immediately obvious that Mark didn't write two discrete sections. He wove them together. The striking of the shepherd and the scattering of the sheep are inextricable.

What is the relationship between them? We've already pondered how Jesus' willingness to die is the cause of the disciples' unwillingness to stick with him. But, gloriously, the opposite is also true. Their unwillingness to stick with him – or, more generally, their failure as disciples, their self-serving, their evil hearts – are the cause of Jesus' willingness to die! He has come to be their Saviour, to give his life as a ransom for friends *who he knows will let him down.*

DIG DEEPER: **'So What?' tool**

What does all of this mean to us? Here are a couple of suggestions that we found online:

> 'Some of the closest companions to Jesus let Him down, yet He was not surprised. It shouldn't surprise us when those closest to us let us down . . . Jesus wasn't surprised when Peter let him down . . . Rejection is a good test of walking in love. What is our response when people reject us, disappoint us?'[4]

> '. . . Peter was unable to keep his promise to Jesus. We must learn from Peter's failure to ensure that, when we promise to do things for friends and relatives, we are in a position to carry through our promises and not let people down. This should be in little things as well as the larger more important life issues.'[5]

Do you think these applications are in line with the author's purpose? If not, why not?

Perhaps you found yourself reaching for the **'Who Am I?' tool**
as you worked through the Dig Deeper exercise. If we are to
apply this passage correctly, we need to ask who in the story
corresponds to whom today. The options are:

1. Peter is like people who upset us.
   We should be like Jesus – we ought to give them a
   second chance.
2. Jesus is like Jesus (i.e. he corresponds to no-one but
   himself).
   We should try to do better than Peter.
3. Jesus is like Jesus.
   Peter is like us – and so we can be wonderfully reassured
   at Jesus' love for him despite everything.

Option (1) makes us uneasy. To read a chapter about the
disciples' failure, and cast yourself as Jesus, the hero? That can't
be right. And the parallels break down when we realize that
we shall never pay a ransom to God for any of our friends. If
anything, option (2) is worse. It's just moralism. And super-
ironic, because on this reading, we are simply repeating Peter's
own sentiment from v. 29!

Option (3) hits the jackpot. We are very like Peter. Regrets
from your non-Christian past are one thing. But the times that
we've let Jesus down *while professing to be his disciples* weigh
even heavier on our consciences. Times we've been ashamed
of him, perhaps – we've not wanted to speak up in defence of
his gospel, or not even wanted to admit that we are Christians.
Times we've done things that (we think) no true Christian would ever have done. Times we think we are beyond
forgiveness. We are so very like Peter.

How comforting to know that Jesus willingly went to his
death for Peter.

Crowned (15:1–39)

Perhaps you've seen *The Iron Lady*, which won Meryl Streep an Oscar for Best Actress. It begins with a row of plastic milk bottles in a corner shop, Indian music playing in the background. An old lady, wearing a drab raincoat and headscarf, chooses a pint of semi-skimmed and walks falteringly towards the counter. Another customer pushes past her. She asks the price – 49p – and raises an eyebrow. She exits onto a busy London street, and dodders along, blue plastic bag in hand.

The film is about Margaret Thatcher, one of the most powerful women in British history. But the opening sequence is clever, because she doesn't look like a powerful woman. She looks senile and frail. We don't at first recognize her for who she is (or was).

This penultimate chapter of Mark's Gospel is all about Jesus as King. The title: 'King of the Jews / Israel' comes no fewer than six times (**Repetition tool**). And yet, as he is whipped and mocked and led away to execution, he looks nothing like a king. We don't at first recognize him for who he is.

'Are you the King of the Jews?'

The chapter begins with Jesus before the Roman governor, Pilate, for a rerun of his earlier trial before the Jewish council. The **Context tool** prompts us to compare the two, and we find several striking similarities.

	Jesus before the Council (14:53–65)	Jesus before Pilate (15:1–15)
The key question	'Are you the Christ, the Son of the Blessed?'	'Are you the King of the Jews?'
Jesus' response	'I am'	'You have said so'
The other questions	'Have you no answer to make? What is it that these men testify against you?'	'Have you no answer to make? See how many charges they bring against you'
Jesus' response	But he remained silent and made no answer	But Jesus made no further answer, so that Pilate was amazed

So, the trial once again reveals that Jesus is innocent of all charges except his claim to be King. Perhaps, the chief priests hope, even this will be enough to convict him in a Roman court, because of the implicit threat the title poses to Caesar's rule. But Pilate isn't fooled for a second. Seeing through their motives (**Linking Words tool**, 15:10), he tries repeatedly to have Jesus released.

Mark highlights Jesus' innocence further by telling us about Barabbas, 'who had committed murder in the insurrection' (v. 6) – i.e. who was *actually* guilty of trying to overthrow the Romans. Pilate has rightly convicted him, but now he is released, and Jesus is condemned. The innocent is punished, and in direct consequence, the guilty goes free. Is there a note here of substitution, for which Mark has already prepared us back in 10:45?

Who is responsible, though, for the miscarriage of justice that sees Jesus sentenced to death? Pilate, although supposedly in charge, comes across as entirely passive: a weak man who bows to peer pressure. It's easier to lay the blame at the feet of the chief priests. They've been conspiring against Jesus for most of the Gospel, and now they get their chance to move in for the kill. But when we use the **Context tool**, it's the crowd who surprise us the most. They have been Jesus' fans throughout the Gospel, even as the establishment rejected him:

> [T]he chief priests and the scribes . . . were seeking a way to destroy him, for they feared him, because all the crowd was astonished at his teaching.
>
> (11:18)

> [T]hey were seeking to arrest him but feared the people [literally, 'the crowd'].
>
> (12:12)

But when Pilate asks the crowd what he should do with 'the man you call King of the Jews?', they shout for him to be crucified. All of them are complicit in the murder. They don't recognize him as King now.

As we move from Jesus' trial to the crucifixion itself, we find people who *do* acknowledge Jesus as a king. They dress him accordingly, in a purple robe. He is given a crown. Soldiers bow before him in homage. 'Hail, King of the Jews!' they say (15:16–20). But this is sarcasm. The crown is woven from thorns. They spit and strike him as they bow. His 'kingship' is, for them, a huge joke.

Then he is nailed to the cross, 'And the inscription of the

charge against him read, "The King of the Jews"' (v. 26). Mark doesn't miss an opportunity to remind us of his central theme.

Then the chief priests, formerly so outraged at Jesus' 'blasphemy' at daring to call himself the Christ, now happily address him by the same title. 'He saved others; he cannot save himself. Let the Christ, the King of Israel, come down now from the cross that we may see and believe' (vv. 31–32). What fun to ridicule him, now that no-one could take his claims seriously.

Imagine that your only view of Jesus came from this chapter (as if your only knowledge of Margaret Thatcher derived from the episode in the corner shop). What would you make of him?

'Surely this man was the Son of God'

In at least three different ways, Mark shows us that Jesus really is God's Christ. Those who used the title in jest did not realize how truly they spoke. Indeed, he's not King *despite* the suffering he endures, but rather King *because* of it. The crucifixion is his coronation.

First, consider the words of his executioner:

> [W]hen the centurion, who stood facing him, saw that in this way he breathed his last, he said, 'Truly this man was the Son of God!' (v. 39)

We're not told exactly how he infers this from the manner of Jesus' death. But this time, we can be sure that there is no hint of sarcasm. Indeed, thanks to Mark's *Columbo*-style preview back in 1:1, we recognize this as one of the two most significant confessions of faith in the whole Gospel.

Secondly, we see Jesus' own predictions about the 'Son of Man' – that most glorious of all kingly titles – fulfilled (**Context tool**):

[T]he Son of Man will be delivered over to the chief priests and the scribes, and they will condemn him to death and deliver him over to the Gentiles [i.e. Pilate]. And they will mock him and spit on him, and flog him and kill him. And after three days he will rise.

(10:33–34).

Thirdly, Jesus' dying words make the same point, albeit in a subtle way that modern readers easily miss. If someone mentions 'Hark! The Herald Angels Sing', then you know that they are talking about the Christmas carol, because we refer to songs by their first line. So, how come we don't spot that when Jesus says, 'My God, my God, why have you forsaken me?' (15:34), he is talking about Psalm 22? Time to do some digging.

DIG DEEPER: **Quotation/Allusion tool**

What similarities can you find between the psalmist's experience and that of Jesus in Mark 15? (Hint: take a look at vv. 1, 7–8, 16 and 18.)

Noticing similarities is not enough. We need to discover the significance.

- Who wrote the psalm? How does that help us understand what we are seeing in Mark 15?
- How does the psalm end (vv. 19–31)? How does that anticipate the events of Easter morning?

Try to summarize how Psalm 22 has helped you understand Mark 15.

Hopefully, you saw from Psalm 22 that suffering is not intrinsically un-royal. David, the greatest king of the Old Testament, suffered.[2] And so did Jesus. But can we go further and ask why?

One striking detail comes in Mark 15:33: there was darkness in the middle of the day for three hours. I (Andrew) remember rushing down to Cornwall in the summer of 1999, armed with my pinhole camera, to catch a glimpse of the solar eclipse. It was eerie. At ten past eleven, bright Cornish sunshine. At eleven minutes past, total darkness. It became suddenly cold. The birds abruptly stopped singing. On the day that Jesus died, it was like that, but for three hours. A supernatural turning-off of the sun on the (literally) darkest day of history.

To understand what this means, we need the **Context tool**. Only a few days previously, Jesus had spoken of a day when 'the sun will be darkened, and the moon will not give its light' (13:24). When we discussed this verse earlier, we disagreed with Professor Bolt in his suggestion that it referred to the crucifixion. No, we said, the context makes clear that this verse is about God's final judgment on the whole world. But the Professor was on to something: although (we still think) Mark 13:24 wasn't referring to the cross, the events of the cross *do* refer to Mark 13:24! The darkening of the sun as Jesus dies is an anticipation of the darkening of the sun on judgment day. Some of God's anger, stored up for the final day of reckoning, is being poured out in advance.

With whom is God angry? Certainly the Jewish authorities, who are murdering his Son. This is clear from the way in which God, in judgment, rips up the curtain in their temple. Perhaps we've surprised you, because your instinctive interpretation of the ripped curtain is that Jesus' death gives us open access to the Most Holy Place where God dwells. That is what Hebrews 10:19–22 has to say about it. But before we allow ourselves to go on theological autopilot, we need to remember the **Author's Purpose tool**. What if Mark is making a different point from Hebrews? He has had lots to say about the temple already, but all in the context of judgment. Like the fig tree, it will wither (11:12–20). There 'will not be left . . . one stone upon another that will not be thrown down' (13:2). Sandwiched in between these prophecies of doom came Jesus' exposition of the reason for them: the wicked tenants were about to kill the Son of the vineyard owner (12:1–12), and in reply, God would 'destroy the tenants and give the vineyard to others'. The fullness of this judgment wasn't due for another forty years, but the supernatural ripping of the curtain at the exact time at which they perform the murder would seem to be a sign of God's terrible anger at what they have done.[3]

However, it is not just the Jews who are on the receiving end of God's anger. Jesus' cry, 'My God, my God, why have you forsaken me?', shows that he too, the beloved Son of God, is enduring the wrath of God. As readers of Mark, this is a bittersweet moment. How terrible, and yet how wonderful. Jesus drinks from the cup he had so feared, so that we might not have to. He offers his life as our ransom. He dies as our Passover lamb, so that God's judgment will pass over us.

Consider the poignant irony in the chief priests' words: 'He saved others; he cannot save himself' (15:31). On the contrary, he could so easily have saved himself. The one who calmed seas and rebuked evil spirits, who multiplied loaves and opened blind eyes? To come down from the cross would have been easy. But, had he saved himself, he would not have saved others. And that is what he came to do.

What a King!

He has risen (15:40 –16:8)

Both of us have had the privilege, in recent years, of helping with university missions. Thanks to the work of UCCF (the Christian Union movement), students are increasingly trained in 'apologetics' – which isn't about saying sorry, but rather about offering a reasoned defence of the gospel (the Greek word *apologia* means 'defence', e.g. Acts 22:1; Philippians 1:16). This can only be a good thing. As the so-called New Atheists go on the rampage, spouting all kinds of nonsense, it's right that we fight back with topics like: 'New Evidence the Gospels were Based on Eyewitness Accounts', or 'Why Atheists are Bad Scientists'. (The latter title got me, Andrew, into quite a lot of trouble, but God was gracious enough to bring people to hear the gospel anyway!)[1]

We need to be careful, though, that we don't put more confidence in our arguments than in the Bible itself. It's easy to let our opponents set the terms of the debate, so that we engage in combat using only their weapons. They choose a 'persuasive speaker', so we try to find a 'more persuasive speaker'. They cite philosophers, so we cite more philosophers. But because they are reluctant to open the Bible with us, and read a paragraph in context, we are reluctant to do so with them. That seems crazy. Can you imagine Luke Skywalker fighting one of the monsters in Jabba the Hutt's dungeon with his bare fists, and forgetting the light sabre in his pocket?! And there we are, with 'the sword of the Spirit, which is the word of God' (Ephesians 6:17) . . . and we don't use it?

Conversely, I (Andrew) recently heard an evangelistic talk that was absolute genius. Not only was it ruthlessly logical, but it had different things to say to different groups in the audience, so that no-one escaped the impact. But just before I hailed the preacher as the most brilliant apologist of our day, I realized what he'd done. He had simply worked through Luke 7, digging deeper to get to the heart of what Jesus was saying, and had given us that. How wise of the preacher to recognize that the Holy Spirit was a better apologist than he was, and to plagiarize his entire message from the inspired Word of God!

We would love to hear more evangelistic talks on suffering taken directly from (for example) Luke 13:1–17, more Other Religions talks taken from John 13:36 – 14:11, and more Resurrection talks taken from Mark 15:40 – 16:8! For the fact is, as we dig into this final part of Mark's Gospel, we shall find that he engages in apologetics. To convince us of the resurrection, he persuades us that Jesus had been really dead. And that afterwards, he was really alive.

Really dead

Mark's first step is to introduce some key witnesses: Mary, another Mary and Salome. Apparently, they've been around from the start (15:41), but we haven't really noticed them before.[2] So, why introduce them now? The **Context tool** reminds us that the primary witnesses, the apostles, have fled the scene, and so these women fill the vacuum. They watch only 'from a distance' – a phrase that reminds us rather poignantly of Peter back in 14:54. But their role is crucial: as eyewitnesses, they assure us that Jesus was dead and buried.

Mark's apologetic is more extensive, however. Using the **Structure tool**, we notice that the account of Jesus' burial is carefully constructed around no fewer than three sets of witnesses. One is a high-ranking Jew (a 'respected member of the Council', 15:43), and one is the Roman governor. You couldn't wish for higher-profile testimony:

> Women observe Jesus' death
>> Joseph asks for the body
>>> Pilate verifies Jesus' death
>> Joseph lays Jesus in a tomb
> Women observe the burial

The structure hinges around Pilate: before sanctioning the burial, he specifically checks with the centurion in charge of the execution that Jesus has died, to make absolutely sure. A subtle change in vocabulary underlines the verdict: in v. 43, Joseph asks for the 'body', but in v. 45, he is given the 'corpse'. (We might add that Joseph, while wrapping Jesus in a shroud, would have had every opportunity to notice shallow breathing or other signs of life. The one thing you don't do to someone you respect is seal him in a tomb with lingering doubts that he might still be alive.)

Thus, Mark puts the final nail in the coffin (to pick an appropriate metaphor) of the so-called 'swoon theory'. The idea that Jesus simply fainted on the cross, only to regain consciousness in the tomb, and thus persuade his disciples that he had risen, begins to sound ridiculous. It flies in the face of the evidence.

If you've spoken to Muslim friends, you may know that the Qur'an also attempts to write Jesus' death out of history:

And [for] their saying, 'Indeed, we have killed the Messiah, Jesus, the son of Mary, the messenger of Allah.' And they did not kill him, nor did they crucify him; but [another] was made to resemble him to them. And indeed, those who differ over it are in doubt about it. They have no knowledge of it except the following of assumption. And they did not kill him, for certain.

(Qur'an 4:157–158)

The problem is that Muhammad wrote more than 500 years after the events, with no access to the eyewitnesses. When we look at the first-century text of Mark, there seems to be rather less 'doubt' and 'assumption' than he claims. Jesus really was dead.

Really alive

The story continues with the two Marys and Salome rushing to the shops on Saturday night (the Sabbath trading restrictions ended at nightfall) to buy the spices needed to anoint Jesus' body as soon as possible (i.e. at dawn). Bearing in mind that the original manuscript included no chapter divisions, 16:1 follows very strangely indeed from 15:47. You'd expect Mark to say, 'When the Sabbath was past, *they* . . .', but instead, he gives us their names again in full. The **Author's Purpose tool** makes us ask why. Surely he is rubbing our noses in the fact that the women who saw Jesus buried (15:47) are the same as the women who were about to find the tomb empty (16:1). There is continuity. And so, as a master apologist, Mark closes the door on the 'they-went-to-the-wrong-tomb' theory.

Then there is Mark's record of the women's conversation, as they belatedly realize that the stone sealing the tomb will scupper their plan to anoint Jesus' body. Again, this material is important from an apologetics standpoint, because Mark subtly underlines that a resurrection *was not what the women were expecting*. Out with the 'they-hallucinated-what-they-were-predisposed-to-believe' theory.

When they arrive and find the stone rolled away, Mark pauses to tell us that 'it was very large' (v. 4). Not good news for the 'the disciples-stole-the-body' theory.

Then we come to the climax of the chapter, as God's messenger gives the most important press release in history. It is not enough that the women should be told, 'He has risen.' They are also directed to evidence to back this up: the empty tomb ('See the place where they laid him', v. 6), and an imminent encounter with the risen Jesus in Galilee ('you will see him', v. 7).

Some modern sceptics protest that no amount of evidence would suffice to convince them of something as 'improbable' as the resurrection. But the term 'improbable' is almost meaningless, because it depends so much on a person's pre-suppositions. If there were no God, if the laws of biology as we observe them must always hold (and that's a big 'if' – science itself can't prove an 'always' from a 'whenever we've checked'), if Jesus were no more than a deluded religious fanatic . . . then a resurrection would seem unlikely. But if there is a God who rules the universe, if the laws of biology as we observe them are no more than a description of the consistent way in which he ordinarily chooses to sustain the world, if Jesus is his Son, authenticated already by many other miracu-lous displays of power . . . then it's staying dead in a tomb that begins to look like an implausible outcome. Anyone prepared to accept even the possibility of the second set of presuppos-itions would have to acknowledge that it makes much more sense of the evidence that Mark gives us. Jesus was really dead. Three days later, he was really alive. And the alternative theories stack up about as well as a Jenga tower built from spherical pieces sprayed with WD-40 in a high wind.

Really important

We've seen that Mark wants us to be sure about what happened that first Easter. But as we continue to dig deeper, we shall discover that he also wants to show us what it means theologically, and how we should respond. Sometimes our resurrection apologetic ends merely with an appeal to 'believe that it happened'. But Mark wants much more from us than that.

The key to understanding the resurrection theologically is the **Context tool**. We need to understand it in light of the whole Gospel story, and see how it brings to a climax themes that Mark has been working with for some time. In particular, we shall see that (putting on our preacher's hats and going for the alliteration): 'Resurrection means Reconciliation', 'Resurrection means Retribution', and 'Resurrection means Risk is Right'.[3]

It was the angel's words: 'just as he told you' (16:7) that put us on to the first theme. Clearly, Jesus' forthcoming appearance at Galilee is to be understood in the context of something he had previously said:

> And Jesus said to them, 'You will all fall away, for it is written, "I will strike the shepherd, and the sheep will be scattered." But after I am raised up, I will go before you to Galilee.' Peter said to him, 'Even though they all fall away, I will not.' And Jesus said to him, 'Truly, I tell you, this very night, before the cock crows twice, you will deny me three times.'
> (14:27–30)

Shortly after that conversation, we saw every single one of the disciples abandon Jesus. Now the sheep scattered at the cross are to be gathered to the risen King.[4] They let him down so, so badly. But he paid a ransom for them, and now he prepares to welcome them back as his beloved friends.

Notice how Peter is singled out: 'Tell his disciples and Peter' (16:7). Strictly speaking, the last two words are unnecessary, because Peter was a disciple. But, of course, he was the one who let Jesus down in the most personal, awful way. How beautiful that the angel should specify Peter as one whom Jesus, in his grace, was especially keen to meet.

I (Tim) vividly remember the first World Cup I ever got to watch. It was France '98, when David Beckham famously aimed a petulant kick at an Argentinian opponent. He received a red card, England went on to lose the match, and Beckham became Public Enemy Number One. But imagine instead if the tabloids had printed this headline the next day: 'To the England football team *and Becks* – we forgive you'. That would have been a particular comfort to the guy who had brought so much disgrace on himself. What consolation there is for sinners in the resurrection of Jesus. Resurrection means Reconciliation.

Secondly, Resurrection means Retribution. These two ideas were placed side-by-side back in 12:1–12, when Jesus warned that God would 'destroy the tenants' (retribution) and that 'The stone that the builders rejected has become the cornerstone' (resurrection). But the connection becomes clearer when we remember Jesus' warnings that the Son of Man himself would be the agent of God's judgment when he 'comes in the glory of his Father' (8:38), when they see him 'coming in clouds with great power and glory' (13:26; see also 14:62). A Jesus who remains buried in a tomb presents no threat to his enemies. But one who has smashed through death will surely return to settle the score.

Thirdly, Resurrection means Risk is Right (or Self-denial is Sensible). We thought we'd leave this one to you.

DIG DEEPER: **Context tool** and **'So What?' tool**

Reread 8:31–38. What is Jesus asking of his disciples? How does his own resurrection act as a key motivation? (Perhaps the following diagram might jog your memory.)

Assuming that you felt the challenge of Jesus' teaching back in chapter 8, and resolved to put it into practice, now is a good time to take stock and ask if you've made any progress. How does this climax to the Gospel spur you on?

Spend some time meditating (we don't mean sitting with your legs crossed, humming, and unscrewing tiny imaginary light bulbs with each hand; we mean meditation in the Psalm 1:2 sense) as follows:

'I find it hard to deny myself in the area of _____. But Jesus rose again. That means _____ (fill in the blanks).

Really strange ending

Mark's Gospel ends very abruptly: 'And they went out and fled from the tomb, for trembling and astonishment had seized them, and they said nothing to anyone, for they were afraid' (16:8). It's such an odd ending that various scribes in the early centuries tried to help by adding a few paragraphs of their own, which appear in your Bible as vv. 9–20. These aren't included in the earliest surviving manuscripts of Mark's Gospel (e.g. Codex Sinaiticus, which you can see for free in the British Library), and that's a sure sign that they are not original. Mark himself wanted to end at v. 8.

(Don't be freaked out by this. There are only two places in the whole of the New Testament where something substantial got inserted later – the other is John 7:53 – 8:11. Neither represents a shift in Christian doctrine, and both are flagged up very clearly in modern Bibles. The remarkable thing is actually how *little* variation there is between different manuscripts of the New Testament, and how very carefully the text was copied.)

Having seen that Mark's Gospel ends at 16:8, we need to reach for the **Author's Purpose tool** for the last time and ask *why*. Why did Mark want such an abrupt ending?

The first thing that must be said is that Mark's ending seems historically honest. If you were writing a fairy-tale Gospel, this is the point where the ladies would break into song, accompanied by the angel on his harp. Only someone wanting to record facts would dare to give us such an anticlimax as: 'they were scared and ran'.

Perhaps the **Context tool** can help us further, because this isn't the first time that Jesus' followers have responded to him in fear. In our study of 4:35 – 6:6, we noted that fear of Jesus can be very positive, for it is an acknowledgment of how awesomely powerful he is. A Jesus who calms a storm is not merely a 'mate', but a Messiah. A Jesus who comes back from the grave is not someone you take lightly, but a King at whose feet you fall trembling. It is right to fear Jesus in precisely the same way that the whole of the Bible tells us that it is right to fear God (e.g. Genesis 22:12; Psalm 36:1; Proverbs 1:7; 1 Peter 2:17; Revelation 14:7).

But we also noted previously that fear of Jesus can combine with unbelief. The residents of the Decapolis witnessed Jesus' terrifying power over demons, but begged him to leave them alone.

How, then, should we assess the women's response of fear at the resurrection? If we use the **Linking Words tool** to unpack Mark 16:8, we find that their fear gives rise to two negative responses. First, they 'fled' (compare 14:50 and 14:52 and, perhaps most tellingly of all, 5:14). Secondly, they kept silent, despite being instructed specifically to go and tell.

We can understand the women being frightened. Indeed, we'd be suspicious if they weren't. The news that Jesus has smashed through death should make anyone tremble. But we can't be satisfied by what they do with their fear. We want to see awe-inspired obedience, reverent joy. We want to read of the smile on Peter's face as they tell him, and the subsequent proclamation of this glorious gospel 'to all nations' (cf. 13:10). Of course, we can read of these things in the other Gospels and in the book of Acts. But we don't read them in Mark. Instead, he puts down his pen and rolls up his papyrus. He wants the ending to dissatisfy. He wants us to refuse to accept that this can be the end. He wants us, in our frustration at the women, to resolve ourselves to respond better to this news. He wants us to go into all the world, as transformed people, to proclaim the gospel joyfully.

Heavenly Father, thank you for teaching us the gospel of Jesus Christ, the Son of God, and for opening our eyes to see. Thank you for giving us a glimpse in history of the wonderful kingdom that Jesus will one day usher in – no evil, no sickness, no sin – and thank you that we can be members of this kingdom through his death and resurrection. We praise you for the ransom he paid, the cup he drank, the blood he shed, so that you would pass-over us on the day of judgment. We ask for grace to repent and believe. To be willing, each day, to deny ourselves, take up our cross and follow him. To have in mind always the hope of glory ahead, the certain hope of resurrection. Amen.

Appendix 1: Is Mark history?

'No-one knows who the four Gospel writers were,' writes
Richard Dawkins in *The God Delusion*. It's the kind of assertion
that makes atheists smile and Christians look sheepish – that
is, unless either does any actual research. Then we discover
that Dawkins is bluffing. Consider the testimony of Papias, a
Christian in the second century:

> Mark, having become the interpreter of Peter, wrote down
> accurately, though not in order, whatsoever he remembered of
> the things said or done by Christ. For he neither heard the Lord
> nor followed him, but afterward, as I said, he followed Peter, who
> adapted his teaching to the needs of his hearers, but with no
> intention of giving a connected account of the Lord's discourses,
> so that Mark committed no error while he thus wrote some things
> as he remembered them. For he was careful of one thing, not to
> omit any of the things which he had heard, and not to state any
> of them falsely.[1]

So Papias, writing not long after Mark's Gospel was first circu-
lated, seems to know exactly who the author was! The purpose
of this short appendix is to increase your confidence in the
Gospel as eyewitness testimony, and thereby equip you to
engage with sceptical friends.

Did Mark write the truth?

When I (Andrew) get talking about these things to atheists in the pub, I try to make two points: Mark's Gospel is not the sort of story that you *would* make up, and it's not the sort of story that you *could* make up.

When I say that it's not the sort of story you *would* make up, I mean that someone trying to invent a popular religion could do a lot better. For example:

- Roman occupation was tremendously unpopular in the first century, and the Jews sought a Messiah who would lead them in revolt. But Mark gave them one who befriends tax collectors (2:14), and even tells people to pay their taxes (12:17).
- The early church was founded on the teaching of the apostles. It matters that they were credible leaders. But Mark openly admits that one of them was so cowardly that he denied Jesus before a servant girl (14:66–72).
- Jesus' crucifixion was always going to be a major obstacle to Jews becoming Christians. They knew from Deuteronomy 21:23 that someone hanged on a tree was under the curse of God, and so reasoned that he could not be the Messiah.[2] Similarly, pagans found the crucifixion laughable. A piece of ancient graffiti discovered in Rome depicts a Christian named Alexamenos worshipping a 'god' with a donkey's head, hanging on a cross. But rather than playing down this aspect of Jesus' story, Mark makes it the centrepiece of his account.

It's not the sort of story that Mark *could* make up, because he describes public events, and is specific about names and places. Everyone knows that fairy tales begin: 'Long long ago, far far away . . .' The advantage of such stories is that no-one can check. If I (Tim) told you that I once levitated a fox for twenty-five seconds while alone in an unspecified forest, you'd have to take my word for it. The same goes for Muhammad's claim that he met the angel Gabriel in a cave and received the Qur'an. But Mark specifies that Jesus healed huge crowds at Capernaum and Gennesaret (1:21–34; 6:53–56), that he raised from the dead the daughter of a man named Jairus, a synagogue ruler (5:22), that the man who carried his cross was 'Simon of Cyrene' (15:21). It's easily *checkable*. If untrue, it is easily debunked. Mark's first readers have only to go to Capernaum and ask around. They can interview Jairus or Simon. And if they can't find Simon, they can ask his sons, because Mark adds that he was 'the father of Alexander and Rufus': it's hard to see why this could be relevant other than that these boys were well known in the early Christian community, and therefore could be sought out for testimony.

If you're willing to do some reading at a more academic level, we'd highly recommend *Jesus and the Eyewitnesses* by Richard Bauckham (Eerdmans, 2006). Among his many fascinating and compelling arguments, he shows that people in the Gospels and Acts have the right names, and in the right proportion, for people living in first-century Palestine. It turns out that there are eight different men named Simon / Simeon, six Josephs, five Johns, five Judases, but (for example) only one Nicodemus. When we compare this to a database of 3,000 Palestinian Jewish names, taken from burial inscriptions and the like, we discover that the most popular name of the day was Simon / Simeon, followed by Joseph, then Lazarus, Judas and John. The rankings are almost an exact match. This is unsurprising, of course, if Mark is writing real history, and calling people what they were actually called. But imagine he's writing a fictitious Gospel from one of the places that Christianity later became established, where different names were in vogue; in Egypt, for example, the Jewish maternity wards were awash with Eleazars and Sabbataiuses, with not a Simon to be seen. How on earth could Mark have guessed the right names for his fictional characters, let alone get them in the right ratio? The eyewitness explanation makes much more sense.

Wasn't there a conspiracy about which Gospels were 'chosen'?

Dan Brown's bestseller, *The Da Vinci Code*, popularized the conspiracy theory that the fourth-century Roman Emperor Constantine censored various alternative Gospels in favour of the four whose version of Jesus he happened to prefer. Matthew, Mark, Luke and John have come to be more 'official', but aren't necessarily more historical, Brown suggests.

There are a number of reasons why this is nonsense. First, there is evidence that the early church (long before Constantine) knew of only four Gospels. The second-century bishop Irenaeus famously wrote:

> It is not possible that the Gospels can be either more or fewer in number than they are. For, since there are four zones of the world in which we live, and four principal winds . . . it is fitting that [the Church] should have four pillars . . . He who was manifested to men, has given us the Gospel under four aspects.
> (*Against Heresies*, 3.11.8)

When the second-century writer Tatian wanted to compile material from all of the Gospels into a single narrative, known as the *Diatesseron*, he used only the traditional four. The Muratorian Fragment, thought to be the earliest list of New Testament books, refers only to the traditional four. And so on.

Secondly, the alternative Gospels, such as Thomas, Philip or Mary, are demonstrably fakes. They date from the mid-second century onwards, and so by definition contain no useful eyewitness material. They mention hardly any place names, because their authors had never been to Israel. In the passage about paying taxes to Caesar, Thomas drops a clanger by mentioning a gold coin, whereas Mark correctly refers to the denarius (made of silver). Theologically, they are out of step with the rest of the New Testament, being preoccupied with the need for the soul to escape the physical body – this was a popular Greek idea that Paul explicitly refutes in 1 Corinthians.

Thirdly, Dan Brown's specific suggestion that the biblical Gospels are anti-women, and that the Gnostic Gospels restore the balance, shows he has read neither! Some of the greatest heroes in Mark are women – the Syrophoenician (7:24–30), the widow in the temple (12:41–44), the woman who anoints Jesus (14:3–9). Conversely, it's hard to find a more misogynistic statement than that which closes the Gospel of Thomas:

> Simon Peter said to Him, 'Let Mary leave us, for women are not worthy of Life.' Jesus said, 'I myself shall lead her in order to make her male, so that she too may become a living spirit resembling you males. For every woman who will make herself male will enter the Kingdom of Heaven.'
> (v. 114)

Oh dear!

Doesn't Mark contradict Matthew, Luke and John?

Another favourite weapon in the sceptic's arsenal is the issue of alleged contradictions between the four Gospels. So you're telling a colleague about, say, the man who lived among the tombs, from whom Jesus drove out 2,000 demons (oink-splosh), and she points out gleefully that in Matthew's account there are *two* demon-possessed men (Mark 5:1–20; Matthew 8:28–34). What are we to make of that?

Ironically, what your colleague sees as a problem could actually be considered a real advantage. From a historian's point of view, it's much better to have two accounts of the same event than one. And it's precisely the discrepancies between them that persuade experts that they are dealing with independent sources. One of our barrister friends was recently working on a public inquiry into the British Army's conduct in Iraq, for which he interviewed 221 soldiers. The experience strengthened his faith in the Gospels, he says, as he gained a fuller understanding of how eyewitness testimony works. A particular soldier's testimony would often differ from others in minor details, and there were even apparent contradictions that, on further investigation, proved resolvable. Indeed, the one thing that would make him really suspicious, he said, would be two accounts that came out verbatim: that would be evidence of collusion.

If you want to do some further reading, we'd highly recommend *Inerrancy and the Gospels* by Vern Poythress (Crossway, 2012). He looks at various alleged contradictions and how we might resolve them, for example:

- If there were two demon-possessed men in the region of the Gerasenes (Matthew), then it's perfectly acceptable for Mark to focus in and tell the story of one of them. At no point does he specify that there was 'only one'.
- When Mark tells us that Jesus met Bartimaeus 'as he was leaving Jericho' (10:46), but Luke says the encounter took place 'as he drew near to Jericho' (18:35), it's possible that they are referring to different places: the

site of the ancient city of Jericho (from Joshua's time) was just outside the first-century city of the same name. By analogy, the statement: 'Tim lives in the City of London' need not contradict: 'Tim rode his Vespa from home into the City of London', if the first is written by a Yorkshireman who uses the term to refer to the whole metropolis, and the second by a Londoner for whom it denotes only the Square Mile around St Paul's.

The biggest help of all, as we puzzle over why Mark narrates a particular episode differently from Luke or Matthew, is the **Author's Purpose tool**. What if Mark, under the inspiration of the Holy Spirit, intended to pick up a different emphasis? Our hearts sink when someone pipes up in a Bible study to inform the group of some extra details in Luke that might help us to understand Mark. It suggests that Mark is somehow deficient by himself, and that thanks to our cross-reference column, we can come to his aid. No! What if Mark *intentionally* left out something that Luke chose to put in?[3]

As Jesus dies on the cross, Luke records the words of the centurion in charge of the execution: 'Certainly this man is innocent!' (23:47). Mark reports it differently: 'Truly this man was the Son of God!' (15:39). It's facile to posit a contradiction, because neither Gospel claims to record everything that the centurion said. Each author has been selective, and in Mark's case, he focuses in on the words that underline his central theme: Jesus is the King!

Appendix 2: The Bible Toolkit

Here is a quick recap of the tools introduced in *Dig Deeper: Tools to Unearth the Bible's Treasure* (IVP, 2005).

Author's Purpose tool
The biggest question we can ever ask of a passage in the Bible is simply, 'Why did the author write this?'

Context tool
Words come within sentences, sentences in paragraphs, paragraphs in chapters, chapters in sections . . . If you take a text out of context, you're left with a con!

Structure tool
How has the author broken down his material into sections? How do these sections fit together?

Linking Words tool
Whenever you see a 'therefore', ask what it's there for! And the same goes for words like 'because', 'so that', 'for', etc.

Parallels tool
Bible poetry doesn't tend to rhyme. Instead, it says the same thing twice in different words (and so you get two chances at understanding it): 'Twinkle, twinkle little star; Shiny, shiny, tiny nebular'.

Narrator's Comment tool

Sometimes the author breaks into his narrative to explain what's going on (a kind of 'Pssst, reader, make sure you understand this . . .').

Vocabulary tool

Bible words have Bible meanings. Be alert in case the author is using a familiar word in an unusual way.

Translations tool

Read the passage in more than one translation, just in case there is a nuance that one version has missed.

Tone and Feel tool

Pay attention to how the point is being made. Is it happy? Tragic? Comforting? Frightening? How does the author want you to feel about what he is saying?

Repetition tool

Sometimes the author says something more than once to make sure that we don't miss it. Sometimes the author says something more than once to make sure that we don't miss it.

Quotation/Allusion tool

When the author quotes or alludes to another part of the Bible, we should turn there to see what ideas he is picking up on.

Genre tool

There are many genres in the Bible – e.g. song, historical narrative, genealogy, law. Identifying the genre is important to how we interpret a passage.

Copycat tool

Is the author holding up one of his characters as someone we should imitate, or whose likeness we should avoid?

Bible Timeline tool

Where is this passage on the Bible timeline? Where am I on the Bible timeline? How do I read this in the light of what has happened in between (e.g. the other side of Jesus)?

'Who Am I?' tool

Whose shoes in the passage are we supposed to step into? If any!

'So What?' tool

What implications does this have for me? For my church? For an unbeliever?

Answers

Answers to the Mark familiarity test in 'Getting started'.

1. Jesus is called 'Christ' by: He is called 'Son of God' by:
   Mark the narrator (1:1)   Mark the narrator (1:1)
   Peter (8:29)   God the Father (1:11; 9:7)
   The mocking crowd (15:32) Unclean spirits (3:11; 5:7)
                              The centurion (15:39)

2. 'If anyone would come after me, let him *deny himself and take up his cross and follow me*' (8:34, italics added).

3. Mark refers to twelve apostles (3:14, 16; 4:10; 6:7; 9:35; 10:32; 11:11; 14:10, 17, 20, 43), twelve years (5:25, 42) and twelve baskets (6:43; 8:19).

4. Jesus' instruction to take a moneybag and knapsack comes from Luke 22:36. The other references are from Mark 9:41 and Mark 6:5.

5. The definitive list of animals in Mark is as follows:
camel (1:6; 10:25)	locusts (1:6)	dove (1:10)
wild animals (1:13)	birds (4:4, 32)	pigs (5:11)
sheep (6:34; 14:27)	fish (6:38; 8:7)	dogs (7:27)
worm (9:48)	colt (11:2)	pigeons (11:15)
cock (13:35; 14:30, 68, 72)	lamb (14:12)	

Notes

Getting started

1. You need the **Translations tool** to spot all of these, because the ESV and NIV both switch between 'on the road' and 'on the way', even though it's the same expression in Greek.

The *Columbo* moment (1:1–15)

1. Similar speculations abound when it comes to the duration of Jesus' wilderness trip. Does this correspond to the forty days of rain during Noah's flood (Genesis 7 – 8) or the forty days that Moses spent up Mount Sinai (Exodus 24:18) or the forty days that Goliath faced off the Israelite army (1 Samuel 17:16) or the forty days required for the embalming of Jacob (Genesis 50:3)? The possibilities are almost endless!

2. When you did the Dig Deeper exercise earlier, you might have spotted that Malachi speaks of God's King bringing judgment. This is going to be important later in Mark, but in his introduction, the focus is on Isaiah and the message of salvation (presumably why Mark underlines Isaiah's, rather than Malachi's, contribution in v. 2).

3. Of course, not every imperative in Mark is addressed to us: 'Rise, pick up your bed, and go home' (2:11) was of particular relevance to a certain paralysed man in Capernaum, and the

instructions in 6:7–11 were specific to a particular mission by the apostles and shouldn't necessarily be taken as a blueprint for twenty-first-century evangelism. And yet, these cautions aside, sometimes an imperative is so much in line with Mark's purpose for his readers that we need to do what it says.

The Pharisee-o-meter (2:1 – 3:35)

1. Some take Jesus to be saying: 'The old wineskins of the Old Testament law need to be replaced by the new wineskins of the gospel.' We disagree. As we argue below, there is no reason to think Jesus has any quarrel with the law itself.
2. From the BBC sitcom, *Blackadder Goes Forth*, Episode 3.

A sower went out to sow (4:1–34)

1. This theme is explored in more depth in the 'Plagues' chapter of *Dig Even Deeper*, where we list a few resources for those who want to think further.
2. *Luther's Works*, 51:77.

Scared? (4:35 – 6:6)

1. www.fichier-pdf.fr/2013/08/01/herald-of-free-enterprise-report/preview/page/8 (accessed 13 November 2014).
2. See the appendix 'Commentaries, Copying and Catastrophe' at the end of *Dig Even Deeper*.
3. In fact, the phrase 'they were filled with great fear' in Mark 4:41 uses an expression taken directly from the Hebrew of Jonah 1:16.
4. This concept of a 'fear swap' comes also in 1 Peter, which repeatedly encourages us to 'fear God' (1:17; 2:17), and then tells us not to be afraid of those who persecute us (3:14). Interestingly, Peter decides just before this to quote from Psalm 34, which also bears witness to the fear swap: the psalm expounds the theme of the fear of the Lord (vv. 7, 9, 11), but

was written by David at a time when he was very much afraid of a human enemy (see the heading of the psalm; cf. 1 Samuel 21:12–13).

5. You've got to love Mark's understatement: 'Jesus couldn't do any mighty works here . . . oh, apart from a few people whom he miraculously healed!' We need to remember that Jesus performed miracles primarily to authenticate his teaching (e.g. 2:10–11), and so the point here is not that his power is somehow deficient, but that the people of Nazareth are so incredibly unbelieving that miracles would be a waste of time.

A head on a platter (6:7–30)

1. The **Context tool** backs this up: John was introduced as a preacher of repentance at the very start of the Gospel (1:4).

2. Of course, these connections are not apparent to a first-time reader of Mark, who doesn't yet know what happens in later chapters. But Mark assumes that we shall read him more than once. Only then can we use the **Context tool** at the level of the whole book, rather than just the chapter or paragraph (see the diagram in *Dig Deeper*, p. 40).

Bread of heaven (6:31–52)

1. Don Carson warns that, for the popular commentator William Barclay, 'miracles tend to be lessons *rather than* events' (D. A. Carson, *New Testament Commentary Survey, Fifth Edition*, Leicester: IVP, 2001), p. 30 (italics original). In other words, Barclay wants to draw spiritual applications from something he doesn't actually think happened; he is dealing with a miracle exactly as if it were a parable, and gets zero marks for his use of the **Genre tool**!

2. They are heading to Bethsaida (v. 45) on the north-east shore of the Sea of Galilee, and 'the wind was against them' (v. 48);

therefore the wind must have come from the east, just as in Exodus 14:21.

3. Anyone who has truly embraced the ethos of the *Dig Deeper* books will want to check these connections out for themselves, rather than just taking our word for it. See Exodus 16:1–3, 10, 14, 32 (wilderness); 16:4 (bread from heaven); 18:21, 25 (hundreds and fifties); 14:21–24 (crossing the sea before the morning watch with an easterly wind); 33:19, 22; 34:6 (passing by); 24:12–13, 15, 18 (climbing a mountain to speak with God); 3:14 ('I AM WHO I AM'); 7:13–14, 22, etc. (Pharaoh's heart was hardened).

4. This is an open-ended exercise, and you're welcome to evaluate further possible allusions of your own. We wondered about Psalm 23: 'shepherd', 'green pastures', 'still waters'?

5. To add another layer of complexity, Elijah/Elisha's parting of the Jordan is, of course, also reminiscent of Joshua's parting of the Jordan (Joshua 3). But Joshua's parting of the Jordan is like Moses' parting of the Red Sea.

Heart failure (6:53 – 7:23)

1. BDAG, 3rd edition, p. 508.

2. C. S. Lewis makes a similar point in his essay, *On Forgiveness* (New York: Macmillan, 1960): 'The trouble is that what we call "asking God's forgiveness" very often really consists in asking God to accept our excuses. What leads us into this mistake is the fact that there usually is some amount of excuse, some "extenuating circumstances." We are so very anxious to point these things out to God (and to ourselves) that we are apt to forget the very important thing; that is, the bit left over, the bit which excuses don't cover, the bit which is inexcusable but not, thank God, unforgivable.'

3. Article 20 of the Thirty-Nine Articles of the Church of England.

Crumbs for the dogs (7:24 – 8:10)

1. These cities were located in the province of Syria. The first-century Jewish writer Josephus described the citizens of Tyre as 'notoriously our bitterest enemies' (*Against Apion*, 1.70), and archaeologists tell us that the main temple in Sidon was dedicated to the pagan god Eshmun. Not many Jews here.

2. From the hymn 'Rock of Ages', by Augustus Montague Toplady.

3. Sceptical scholars of a bygone age assumed that such 'doublets' (pairs of accounts that share similarities) came about because Mark was working from various sources, and accidentally included two different versions of the same incident. Oh come on! Give the man some credit! Sadly, those who take such a dismissive approach never bother to use the **Author's Purpose tool** to ask why Mark might have *intended* to narrate two different incidents in a similar way (or why Jesus might have performed two similar miracles for Mark thus to narrate).

4. Indeed, the exodus was foundational to Israel's identity as a nation. See Exodus 19:6.

Unblinded (8:11–30)

1. The metaphor of yeast is used here, as elsewhere in the New Testament, to refer to something that multiplies and spreads (see e.g. Luke 13:21; 1 Corinthians 5:6; Galatians 5:9). Given their obsession with lunch, it's possible that the disciples mishear this as a literal allusion to bread making!

2. Mark ties together the healings of the deaf man in the Decapolis and the blind man at Bethsaida in various ways. In both cases, people 'brought' a man to Jesus and 'begged him' to touch the man; in both, Jesus demands privacy, taking them 'aside from the crowd' or 'out of the village'; in both, Jesus performs the healing using spit; in both, Mark records

the change with a threefold phrase ('his ears were opened, his tongue was released, and he spoke plainly', 'he opened his eyes, his sight was restored, and he saw everything clearly'); in both, Jesus demands that the miracle should not be publicized.

3. From the hymn 'Amazing Grace', by John Newton.

4. From the traditional hymn (author unknown).

Come die with me (8:31 – 9:29)

1. We've spoken before about the need for caution when detecting allusions. The co-occurrence of three relatively common words, 'Son', 'of' and 'Man', in two places in the Bible is not sufficient by itself to establish a link. Why are we sure about it? First, it's not just that the individual words co-occur, but the entire phrase 'Son of Man'. It's an unusual phrase at that. Secondly, the context of Daniel 7, in particular the reference to an everlasting kingdom, fits well with Jesus' proclamations about the kingdom of God. But the clincher is the combination of 'Son of Man' and 'coming in / with clouds' in Mark 13:26 and 14:62 (see Daniel 7:13).

2. There's a well-known Christian song based on this prophecy that gets it a bit muddled. It's a real shame, because the tune is great, and most of the words are great, but . . . can you see the problem? Hint: who is missing? To whom is given, in Daniel, a kingdom that will not pass away? Songwriters, please be careful. Your words stick in our heads, and if you get them a bit wrong, then we learn theology that's a bit wrong.

3. Or one and a half dead guys, for any pedants who remember that Elijah didn't actually die, but 'went up by a whirlwind into heaven' (2 Kings 2:11).

4. Were it not for her commitment to careful Bible-reading, Tim's wife Lucy would be very keen to derive a prohibition on camping from v. 5. She hates camping!

The eye of a needle (9:30 – 10:31)

1. www.reformation21.org/blog/2013/05/when-is-a-book-not-a-book.php (accessed 30 May 2013).

2. If you have time, it would be worth using the **Linking Words tool** to think about the chain of three 'for's in vv. 39–41, and how each stage in the argument backs up Jesus' rebuke of the disciples.

3. The **Parallels tool** reveals an important corrective to those who want to interpret the 'kingdom of God' in this-worldly sociopolitical terms: 'enter the kingdom of God' (v. 47) is in parallel to 'enter life' (vv. 43, 45); the terms are again used interchangeably in 10:17, 23.

4. John Bunyan, *Pilgrim's Progress* (London: Penguin Classics, 2008), p. 46.

5. There are bridges between the three subsections. The first and second contain the phrase: 'it is better' (used in different ways); the second and third are linked by 'salt' (used in different ways).

6. Adultery means person A sleeping with person B, when one of them is already married to someone else. How could this occur after a divorce? Simply because a bit of paper isn't by itself sufficient to dissolve a marriage covenant, and in God's eyes, the couple are still married. However, Matthew's Gospel gives more detail and includes the clause 'except for sexual immorality' (Matthew 19:9; see also Matthew 5:32). Thus, there may be circumstances where a marriage has broken down because of one person's sexual sin, and the innocent party is free to remarry. If you are struggling with these questions, we'd recommend that you speak to those in leadership at your church, so that they can help you.

7. The notion that the eye of the needle was the name of a small gate in Jerusalem that camels could pass through only if stripped of their load (i.e. their riches) is one of those

preachers' stories that has no basis in reality. One scholar, clearly exasperated, explains, 'This door has not in any language been called the needle's eye, and is not so called today' (G. N. Scherer, cited in R. T. France, *The Gospel Of Mark* [Milton Keynes: Paternoster, 2002], p. 405). Jesus' point is not that it's a tight squeeze, but that it can't be done.

A king's ransom (10:32–52)

1. The same transition from talking about Jesus' death as an example for us to follow to speaking about it as a unique act of salvation can be found also in 1 Peter 2:21–25 and 1 John 4:7–10.

2. And readers ought not to worry if they can't work out exactly when they were converted. The sign of having crossed over from death to life is believing in Jesus now. Whether it came about suddenly or gradually, or even as a child so young that you can't remember it, is not important.

3. The observation that the same commandments that are intended to convict us of our sin and throw us on God's mercy can also, for the person who has received mercy, function as a moral guide, is the essence of what Reformed theologians call 'The Third Use of the Law'.

4. From the hymn by Henry Francis Lyte.

Roll out the red carpet (11:1–25)

1. Accordingly, you would also benefit from looking up the context of Isaiah 56:7. You would find that God's original intention for the temple was that it should give people of all nationalities and ethnic backgrounds the opportunity to come to know him. We saw that Jesus has the same concern, when we considered the Syrophoenician woman and the feeding of the 4,000. But, evidently, the corrupt temple authorities did not share this concern.

2. Some have argued that when Jesus speaks of a mountain being thrown into the sea, he is referring to the temple mount. They appeal to the **Context tool** to remind us that pigs were hurled into the sea in judgment back in chapter 5, and now the temple is being judged. Others suppose it to be a reference to the Mount of Olives. Using the **Quotation/Allusion tool**, they dig up Zechariah 14:4 (a few chapters after the colt prophecy), which mentions the Mount of Olives being split in two in order to facilitate salvation. Although both of these are attractive, underlining either the judgment or salvation themes in the chapter as a whole, we think that they may reflect (dare we say) an overenthusiasm for digging deeper! The surface meaning may, in this case, be the best one: if you trust a powerful God, even impossible things become possible.

The stone the builders rejected (11:27 – 12:44)

1. Some try to build an argument from the tense of v. 26 – 'I am the God' rather than 'I was the God' – but this is a mistake, because there is actually no verb in either the Greek of Mark or the Hebrew of Exodus (literally 'I the God of Abraham'). Rather, as we've said, Jesus' logic seems to be that an unfulfilled-in-Abraham's-lifetime promise necessarily implies a beyond-death future. The same kind of reasoning crops up in Hebrews 11:8–16.

The end of the world is nigh (13:1–37)

1. Lewis Carroll, *Alice in Wonderland*, chapter 3.
2. Peter Bolt, *The Cross from a Distance: Atonement in Mark's Gospel* (Leicester: Apollos, 2004).
3. We both found copies in second-hand bookshops, but it's also available for free online. It's recommended reading if you want to get some first-century background.

4. Some get into a muddle, because they confuse the 'abomination' with the destruction of the temple itself. But Mark presents it as an early-warning sign that *precedes* the fall of the temple and the city.

5. R. T. France, *The Gospel of Mark: A Commentary on the Greek Text* (Grand Rapids: Eerdmans, 2002).

6. Compare with the parable of the weeds (Matthew 13:24–30, 36–43), where Jesus describes angels as the reapers at the final judgment (v. 39). It is they who gather the elect for safety (v. 30) and God's enemies for judgment (vv. 30, 41–42).

7. Similar imagery is found in Isaiah 34:4 and Joel 3:15, both of which come in the wider context of universal judgment.

Adored and betrayed (14:1–25)

1. The modern equivalent of 300 denarii (v. 5), taking a denarius as a day's wage on the average UK salary of £517 per week in 2013.

2. Michael Craig-Martin, *An Oak Tree*, 1973. Assorted objects and printed text under glass, 15 × 46 × 14 cm (glass on shelf)/ 30 × 30 cm (text panel). Canberra: National Gallery of Australia (NGA 79.1101). (On loan to the Tate: see www.tate. org.uk/art/artworks/craig-martin-an-oak-tree-l02262.)

3. It's interesting that the blood is for 'many' rather than for 'all' (the same goes for the ransom in 10:45). This is one of several texts that persuade us of what theologians call *particular redemption* or *limited atonement*, namely that Jesus died with the intention of saving his elect specifically.

4. From the hymn 'When I Survey the Wondrous Cross', by Isaac Watts.

The cock crows twice (14:26–72)

1. *Macbeth*, Act 1, scene vii.

2. See Appendix 1: 'Is Mark history?'.

3. Zechariah's prophecy about the striking comes just a few verses after his promise that '[o]n that day there shall be a fountain opened for the house of David and the inhabitants of Jerusalem, to cleanse them from sin and uncleanness' (Zechariah 13:1).

4. 'The Love Test: Meditation for 30th January 2014', http://pastorjerome.org/TipDescription.aspx?tipId=1012 (accessed 4 April 2014).

5. David Shiret, *25 Christian Upper School Assemblies* (Corby: First and Best in Education, 2005), p. 20.

Crowned (15:1–39)

1. www.stepBible.org is like the **Translations tool** on steroids. You click on the word 'crowd' in the ESV, and it searches for the same word *in the underlying Greek text*. This way, we can find places where 'crowd' is used, even when the ESV translated inconsistently.

2. This is clear not only from Psalm 22, to which Mark directs us, but also from the whole narrative of David's life, recorded in 1 and 2 Samuel. An appreciation of the whole sweep of the Bible story always helps our understanding.

3. Perhaps the ethnicity of the centurion provides another subtle link to the parable. Is he, a Gentile, a forerunner of the 'others' to whom the vineyard will be given?

He has risen (15:40 – 16:8)

1. If you're interested in hearing these actual talks, they are available at http://goo.gl/uiXWM4 and http://goo.gl/njLBGQ (accessed 22 May 2014; the last one is a more recent version of the atheists-and-science talk, with a less confrontational title – lesson learned!).

2. Given that the sons of the second Mary have the same names as two of Jesus' brothers (see 6:3), it's possible to infer that this

is Jesus' mother. But those guided by the **Author's Purpose tool** will not want to make a big deal of something that Mark doesn't make a big deal of.

3. The 'Risk is Right' slogan comes from a short book on the same theme by John Piper. It's really good, and available for free download at www.desiringgod.org/books/risk-is-right (accessed 5 June 2014).

4. A few ultra-diligent users of the **Quotation/Allusion tool** may have noticed that even the original 'sheep scattering' quote in Zechariah is followed by a promise of restoration for some:

> They will call upon my name,
>   and I will answer them.
> I will say, 'They are my people';
>   and they will say, 'The LORD is my God.'
> (Zechariah 13:9).

Appendix 1: Is Mark history?

1. Cited by the third-/fourth-century writer Eusebius, *Ecclesiastical History* 3.39.15.

2. See the early second-century document by Justin Martyr, *Dialogue with Trypho, a Jew.*

3. At Bible College, I (Andrew) was urged to buy a 'Synopsis' of the Gospels, which lays them out side-by-side in parallel columns. This can be very helpful for noticing the subtle emphases of each author. The best one to get (and not only because the author has such a corker of a name) is probably *Gospel Parallels: A Comparison of the Synoptic Gospels* by Burton H. Throckmorton, Jr (Thomas Nelson, 1992).

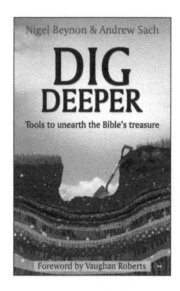

For more information about IVP
and our publications visit

www.ivpbooks.com

Get regular updates at **ivpbooks.com/signup**
Find us on **facebook.com/ivpbooks**
Follow us on **twitter.com/ivpbookcentre**

Inter-Varsity Press, a company limited by guarantee registered in England and Wales, number 05202650. Registered
office IVP Bookcentre, Norton Street, Nottingham NG7 3HR, United Kingdom. Registered charity number 1105757.